THE 10-MINUTE TABLE DECORATOR

Front cover photographs:
(top left) Eaglemoss/Martin Norris; (right/bottom left) Eaglemoss/Gareth Sambidge
Back cover: Eaglemoss/George Taylor

Photographs page 1: Elizabeth Whiting & Associates/Debi Treloar;
page 3: Robert Harding Syndication/Homes & Gardens/Trevor Richards;
page 4: Eaglemoss/Shona Wood;
page 5: Eaglemoss/Laura Wickenden; page 6: Worldwide Syndication/Wohn Idee

Based on *Home Magic, Creative Ideas, Sewing with Confidence;*
pages 9-10 based on *Country Look;* pages 81-84 based on *Creative Hands*

First published in North America
in 1999 by Betterway Books
an imprint of F&W Publications, Inc.
1507 Dana Avenue
Cincinnati, Ohio 45207
1-800-289-0963

ISBN 1-55870-525-2

Printed in Hong Kong

10 9 8 7 6 5 4 3 2 1

THE 10-MINUTE TABLE DECORATOR

BETTERWAY BOOKS
Cincinnati, Ohio

CONTENTS

QUICK TABLE COVERS

UNIQUE NAPKINS

TIME-SAVING CENTREPIECES

Creative Candles

Decorative Tableware and Favours

Table Dressing

Whatever the occasion, set an enticing table with a rich array of fabrics, shapes, colours and styles to flatter your china and add grace and flair to any room.

Whether you're dressing a table for a special occasion, setting a lavish spread for tea in the garden, or simply adding a special touch to a dinner for two – make the most of the opportunity. By choosing carefully, you can dramatically focus attention on the table for a party; achieve a pretty but relaxed al fresco look or add vibrant colour and pattern to the dinner table.

You can find a wide choice of ready-made cloths and covers in department and linen stores, whatever your needs or preferences. But often the most charming arrangements are those you dream up yourself – a piece of antique patchwork draped over a small lamp table, its colours glowing in the light, or a cream voile curtain doing duty on a summer garden table, weighted against the breeze with delicate shells or pearly drops. Sharply tailored covers create a neat, contemporary finish for modern rooms, and can be enlivened with subtle detailing.

Gather a collection of covers that you can use for different occasions – from fringed chenille, through cheery gingham, to crisp white damask or festive red cotton.

▲ ***Boldly bordered*** *A broad red border on this plain cream table cloth picks up the warm, red element of the room scheme, turning the table cover into a distinctive accessory in this smart yet relaxed dining room.*

MEAL TIMES

Specially chosen table coverings and accessories are the perfect way to focus attention on the table, and can add greatly to the enjoyment and character of a meal.

Start the day in cheerful mode with brisk checks or stripes in fresh green and white for summer, or glowing reds and yellows to brighten winter mornings. Busy Provençal prints with their bright, rich colours are ideal; add contrast borders in different but toning colours. Use napkins in plain colours extracted from the tablecloth pattern; choose a different colour for each person. Quilted placemats complete the ensemble. Combine it with chunky terracotta pottery and ceramics in bright colours for a real country farmhouse look.

An old-fashioned afternoon tea offers another chance to create an elegant, refined mood. Choose a plain white cloth embroidered with intricate cups and saucers, or Chinese ladies; overlay a delphinium blue cloth with crunchy white lace and set with classic blue and white china; or try pale green organza appliquéd with trails of red silk strawberries for an indulgent and fanciful strawberry tea. Cut napkins from assorted floral remnants for an old-fashioned country look, combined with dainty floral porcelain on a white cloth.

For formal occasions, nothing beats the sheen of a white-figured damask cloth, set with gleaming gold-banded china and the glitter of silver and crystal. However, there are all sorts of ways to dress up your dinner table and give it an entirely different look. For modern, back-to-nature sophistication, choose natural taupe linen for the cloth, made in a fitted style with narrow black piping; black linen napkins, twisted with raffia, and pristine white china with a wide black band make for an unusual and elegant look. For a festive occasion, choose a centre table runner in gold tissue or organza, strewn with ivy trails and gold ribbon.

Sunshine lunches *Provençal prints are redolent of heady warm days, and blend well together, so you can mix cloth, mats and napkins to create a table sizzling with colour.*

Tea-time delights *A small cloth with subtle white-on-white embroidery layers on the charm over a white damask cloth for a traditional afternoon tea in the garden.*

Eating outdoors

A picnic is one of the most enjoyable ways of getting close to nature. Yet there is no need to foray deep into the backwoods to enjoy the delights of a picnic: just step out into your garden or on to your patio or deck to discover the enchantment of eating amongst the plants and flowers.

You can take the concept of eating outside as seriously as you want. You might, for example, wish to entertain in style, with a full-course dinner, served with wine and lit by candles, oil lamps or flairs. For a daytime party, on the other hand, you could serve a delicious fruity punch with small, tasty snacks, displaying the goodies on a table for the guests to help themselves.

Alternatively, you may wish to make use of an outside table and chairs for informal gatherings with friends or for family meals. Why not lay out a selection of food and drink, hot or cold, for a Sunday brunch or traditional tea. You could even have breakfast here, serving hot frothy coffee and fresh croissants.

Simple pleasures *This simple arrangement of baskets filled with fresh fruit and jars of homemade preserves lets the food be the focal point. The bare, rustic table adds to the country flavour.*

▲ ***Flowers for tea*** *Decorate a tea table in the garden with a lace tablecloth and a vase or jug of fresh flowers. Just pick a bunch of whatever is growing in your garden, like these shoots of blossoming crab apple.*

◄ ***Breakfast special*** *There's no need for flowers on this table surrounded as it is by potted pelargoniums and the flourishing, flower-laden stems of a climbing rose. It's the perfect spot for a late breakfast.*

▼ ***Romantic in pink*** *The scene is set for a romantic evening meal by candlelight. The pink table, flowers and glasses are complemented by the green chairs.*

Cover-ups

A dull, old table can take on a new lease of life with just one simple flourish of fabric. Whether you want to protect the surface of your dining table during meals or dress up a card table to add additional seating at a party, there is a wide choice of style to match your decor and situation.

The easiest way is a loose, throwover style, draped to the floor or hanging in deep points. Imagine the drama of a burgundy velvet cloth with a contrast lining in heavy gold satin, or a knubbly terracotta cotton bordered with figured chenille or tapestry for a medieval look. A small square of red brocade trimmed with corner tassels and spread over a deep blue circular cloth creates an exotic Eastern look under a burnished brass lamp.

For a pared-down, contemporary look, a good choice is a neatly tailored cover that hugs the shape of the table, and falls in a straight, boxy skirt or crisp pleats. Keep it short for convenience on a dining table, so that you can get your knees under the table unimpeded, or to show off elegant tapering table legs. Look for subtle details like striped piping, narrow borders, eyelets and lacing, or bold buttons at corner pleats, and stick to plain, bold colours or restful neutrals.

Textured table cloth *Intricately embellished cutwork is shown to advantage spread over a red undercloth – the pattern underneath only adds to the rich, textured effect.*

Delicate line embroidery *The simplest of embroidered motifs takes a plain cloth out of the ordinary. Here, green ivy worked in chain and stem stitch is ideal for a conservatory table.*

Mix and match *Neat, snappy details bring a floor-length tablecloth bang up to date. Here, a simple fitted cloth is tabbed and buttoned at the corners and bordered at the hem with contrast fabric to tie in perfectly with the rest of the scheme.*

Setting a place

One of the quickest and easiest ways to bring a plain table to life is with a set of decorative placemats.

For a festive mood, choose an exotic fruit pattern in luscious bright colours, or a brilliant Inca-style sun motif in flaming yellows and oranges for a summer breakfast table, and an amusing vegetable print for a lunch table.

Daintily embroidered napkins in fine fabrics add a touch of luxury to a table prepared for a special occasion. Look for colourful, ethnic-style napkins from the Far East or Greece for a contemporary, exotic flavour.

Flowery touches *Use up scraps of multi-coloured floral cotton or linen fabrics by turning them into tea-time napkins to flatter a pretty tea set.*

Fruity mats

This set of circular, fruit-patterned placemats with matching coasters would be perfect for a summer meal by the pool.

A fresh take on quilting *Simple running stitch in black on white sets off white china and sophisticated cutlery. For festive occasions, try gold thread on red, or silver on blue.*

Stylish Place Settings

For stylish dining with family or friends, continue the theme of your chosen room style by selecting table accessories to coordinate with the surrounding decor.

The huge selection of tabletop accessories available makes it easy and fun to select place settings to go with your chosen room style. If you like traditional ideas, then you will be comfortable with crisp white linen, teamed with classic crystal, silverware and china. But if you lean towards a newer, more contemporary style, then you will probably go for bright colours and imaginative designs.

The casual good looks of country tableware are suited to a relaxed and informal way of living. Choose rustic pottery in earth tones, such as those found in French Provençal dishes, chunky wine glasses in coloured glass and knives and forks with contrasting handles. Add cotton napkins with an ethnic print and textured linen placemats in warm, spice tones to complement the dishes.

For a show-stopping, dramatic style table, concentrate on sharp contrasts. Black and white teamed with silver or gold accessories is unbeatable, but other bold primary schemes can be just as eye-catching. Work round the boldest design, balancing a brightly patterned plate, for example, with a plain coloured wineglass and a contrasting plain tablecloth or placemat.

Dramatic impact *Colourful harlequin chequered china set on a bright yellow cloth creates instant drama in this contemporary table setting. Colours for glassware, cutlery and napkins have been chosen to complement the china for maximum impact.*

Contemporary flair *Fresh, spring-like colours and informal checks bring a carefree touch to a soft modern breakfast table. The tableware is simple and unfussy with an absence of pattern. Strict colour matches are irrelevant as the happy mix of accessories works well together in this youthful style, totally geared to modern living.*

Classic chic *A richly polished dining room table is best suited to showing off your finest dinner service and accessories. Here, crisp white linen placemats are set with elegant gold-rimmed plates, silverware and sparkling crystal for a beautiful, traditional look.*

High drama *Create a streamlined dramatic feel with this black and white table setting. An unusual oversized service plate with a cut-out leaf design round the rim is perfectly balanced with a black dinner plate and a giant balloon wineglass.*

Country casual *Capture the charm of warm colour and natural materials with this country look setting. Choose rustic terracotta pots and serving dishes or richly glazed Provençal pottery. Add rush placemats, batik prints and chunky recycled glasses for a homey dining experience.*

Tablecloths and Topcloths

Tablecloths provide a quick and easy way to dress your dinner table for a special occasion. There are a multitude of fabrics and patterns to choose from.

Dressing a table can be as exciting and creative as decorating a room – lace, embroidery, gold lamé, functional stripes and checks, and stunning layers of toning patterns and trimmings are all options to set off a delicious array of appetizers, a sparkling dinner service, or even to serve as magnificent displays in their own right.

Combining two cloths together is a designer trick that's easy to copy. The graceful effect of a circular cloth falling to the floor in elegant folds is accentuated by the corners of a smaller, contrasting cloth laid on top, and falling in points over the longer one. This is a lovely way to display a treasured piece of richly coloured antique tapestry, silk embroidery, or a tasselled shawl against a toning backdrop, or you could even layer three or four coordinating fabrics, one on top of the other, in the colours of your room scheme.

Perfect pairings *Use fabric left over from other soft furnishing projects to make a topcloth for an occasional table. If you don't have enough fabric to reach the floor, layer it over a plain fabric and add toning fringing and chunky tassels.*

Party dressing *A celebratory table with a smart paper cover takes just a few minutes to assemble, and the cover can be thrown away so you don't have to worry about removing stains afterwards. A single, flat piece of paper covers the table top, and the edge is trimmed with a scalloped border strip. Cover the join with a broad strip of gold ribbon.*

Layered look *Use a medley of layered fabrics to turn an occasional table into an eye-catching feature, attracting attention to the items displayed on it. Combine striped, floral and plain fabrics, linking them with a colour theme and edging them all with the same colour binding.*

Leafy appliqué *Appliqué shapes quickly transform a plain tablecloth into a striking focal point. These leaf shapes in pale greens bring a breath of spring to this table setting – it would also make a marvellous picnic cloth. Add a broad, green border for a fresh finishing touch.*

Clever trims

Simple, plain cloths take on a special look with inventive trimmings. Pick a lush fringe in colours that echo your soft furnishings to edge a toning tablecloth, or weight each of the four corners of a topcloth with a silky tassel, or a heavy wooden bead. Stitch a generous sprinkling of sparkling glass beads or gleaming pearls around the edge of a filmy voile cloth and display it over rich blue silk or, for a natural look, dangle dainty shells from the edge of a square of natural linen. Even the addition of ric-rac, linen tape or woven braids can transform the plainest cloth into something out of the ordinary.

Choose edgings and trims to act as colour links: for example, add blue and green trims to a beige linen cloth for a blue and green room scheme.

Celebration style

A gauzy evening fabric, like organza, tied in swags round the side of a velvet cloth, adds a suitably festive feel to a party table setting. Jazz up an ordinary lace cloth by laying it over a length of gold or silver lamé fabric. Paper tablecloths in iridescent or sparkly finishes look good when combined with tissue and crêpe paper for a carefree, throw-away party spread. For a simple look, decorate a plain white paper cloth with gold ribbon or a scattering of gold stars.

Make a point *Bring designer flair to a plain, white topcloth by shaping the hem into sharp points. A striped fabric, neatly mitred at the corners, accentuates the points on this cloth, but you could hang long drops of beads or tassels from the points instead, for an alternative look.*

Golden moments *White lace takes on a decidedly glamorous image when layered over a glittering, gold lamé undercloth that echoes the opulence of all the party trappings – gold-edged glasses, champagne and gilt-wrapped chocolates. Try a lace cloth over a shimmering dark blue or green underlayer for a more restrained way to highlight a lacy design, making it suitable for both formal and informal occasions.*

Display of work *This elegant ensemble combines a pretty cross-stitch cloth in blue and white with a plain blue one. This is an ideal way to display a treasured piece of embroidery – the intricate pattern can easily be seen and admired. Select glassware and table decorations with care, so that they do not detract too much from the charm of the tablecloth.*

The tablecloths you use frequently are likely to need regular laundering, so make sure the fabric is washable and shrinkproof – cotton or linen is ideal. To avoid grease staining the cloth, cover the mark with liquid detergent and wash it as soon as possible. For wine and fruit juices, cover the stain with salt, and rinse in cold water before washing.

Outdoor eating

For outdoor eating you can disguise an old or marked table with an appropriate tablecloth. Checks and stripes are popular, or even a plain white paper tablecloth that can be brightened up with colourful napkins and china, and thrown away afterwards. You can find patterned paper tablecloths to suit most occasions, be it weddings, anniversaries or children's birthday parties.

There are also a wealth of plastic tablecloths available which are particularly suitable for outdoor use, or even for children's parties indoors.

For outdoor eating, go for a cheerful checked or stripey tablecloth to brighten up your garden furniture. A washable fabric is particularly important for casual outdoor settings.

A full-length tablecloth completes a sophisticated dinner party setting. Here, a smart striped fabric matches the chair covers to create a totally coordinated dining scheme.

When choosing a fabric for a tablecloth, bear in mind the style and colour of your room and your tableware. Match the fabric to your decorative scheme, or to your china, placemats or napkins.

If you're short of space when entertaining friends, a folding table makes a useful substitute for a traditional dining table. Disguise it with a boldly patterned tablecloth.

Summer Table Covers

Be creative with your summer tables and dress them with unusual coverings. Choose the most exotic fabrics you can find, and drape, tie or stitch them for dramatic effect.

Whether you are planning a meal for an important celebration and want your table to look extra special, or simply want to liven up an *al fresco* lunch, forget your standard summer cloths and opt for something out of the ordinary. With a little time and thought the simplest tablecloth additions can turn your dining table into something original and exciting.

There is a limitless supply of off-the-shelf items that can be used to brighten up a plain cloth. Different coloured lengths of filmy muslin create a dreamy, romantic look; satin and organza have dramatic appeal, while lengths of simple net tossed over a table can look most effective of all.

If you are dining outside, there are all sorts of tricks you can use to hold your cloth in place. Sew large, bright beads around the edges of a plain cloth, use cloth clips (or painted bull-dog clips) to secure the top of the cloth to the table, or use pebbles – tied to string and draped across the top – for a really breeze-proof table setting.

▲ ***Cover story*** *Transform an old table into a romantic haze of purple with layers of rich, exotic fabrics. Here, a panel of woven organdie ribbon backed with pink satin falls softly over an undercloth of pale lilac. Create a similar effect with lengths of muslin, dyed in exuberant fantasy colours. Jewel-shaded net, too, gives an ethereal feel, which is perfect for summer evening suppers.*

Beach basics *To keep a plastic-coated tablecloth in place during an al fresco meal on a breezy day, scour the shoreline for pebbles with holes. Tie them on to lengths of garden string and lay them across the table. This ingenious idea is practical, and also looks wonderfully in keeping with the beach surroundings.*

Petal strewn *Create a romantic setting for a wedding or anniversary supper by simply draping layers of fine white net over a floor-length white tablecloth, then sewing silk or paper flowers and petals all over it. Tie extra strips of net in bows around the backs of the dining chairs for added elegance.*

Natural edge *Give a contemporary feel to a wooden dining table with linen runners draped lengthways to serve as place settings. Here, the natural look has been accentuated with pots of lush green wheat grass. White tableware has been chosen to keep the look fresh and simple.*

Handpainted Tablelinen

Use fabric paints to apply colourful designs to placemats, tablecloths and napkins, creating your own unique tablelinen. The paints are available in a wide range of colours and can be machine washed.

Fabric paints are ideal for adding instant colour and pattern to plain tablelinen. You can buy them in a wide range of colours, including metallic shades, from craft shops and artists' suppliers. Fabric marker pens are also available, and are useful for outlining designs and adding detailing. The fabric paints can be used right from the bottle or diluted with water to give a softer finish, and you can mix colours to create exactly the desired shade. Some paints need to be heat-fixed by ironing. You can then dry clean or machine wash the item, following the paint manufacturer's instructions.

You can use any design you like for the tablelinen. Fruit and vegetables, and other food-related images are popular, as are flowers and foliage. If the linen is for a special occasion, such as Christmas or a birthday, you can choose the design accordingly – holly leaves and berries, or a collection of gift-wrapped parcels, for example. Abstract designs are quick and easy to paint, and very versatile – a good choice for general-purpose tablelinen that you want to use all year round.

You can use fabric paints on most fabrics, but natural fibres generally give the best results. Keep to pale fabrics so the paint colours show up well – white and cream give the truest colour finish.

▲ *Handpainted vegetables add a colourful finishing touch to this linen placemat. If you are painting a placemat, concentrate the design in one or more corners or round the edges of the mat, rather than in the middle, where it will be obscured by your dinner plate.*

DESIGN IDEAS FOR PAINTED TABLELINEN

Using stencils Stencils are an excellent source of designs for painted tablelinen. Mark through the stencil with a fabric pen or pencil to transfer the design, remove the stencil and hand paint the design using an artists' brush and fabric paint. Add detailing and shading as desired.

Painted borders Instead of painting a corner motif, try painting a border all round the edges of your placemat or napkin. Trace the design before you paint it. The deep hem on the placemat provides a handy guide for keeping the border the same width all round.

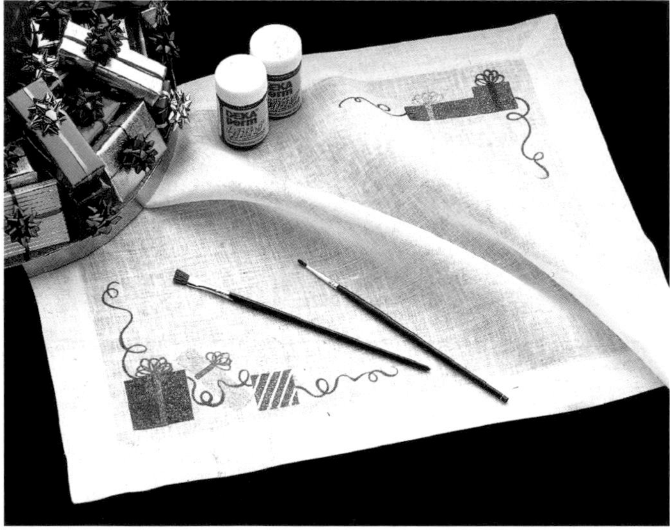

Themed designs If you are decorating tablelinen for a particular occasion, choose a design motif to suit. Here, groups of wrapped gifts suggest a birthday celebration.

Colour hints

- Fabric paints usually dry to a slightly different colour from that of the paint in the pot, depending on your fabric and how thickly you apply the paint. Always test the paint colour on a scrap of the fabric before you begin, and leave it to dry – you can speed up the drying time by using a hairdryer.
- If you need to mix two or three fabric paints to get the colour you want, make sure you mix up enough to complete your project – it's difficult to match a shade exactly the second time round.
- If you want to paint on a dark coloured fabric, you can achieve a truer colour finish by first painting the design in white, leaving it to dry, then painting over it in your desired colours. However, this will give the fabric a stiffer texture. Alternatively, you can mix some white paint in with the coloured paint before you apply it to the fabric – this will lighten the paint, but will also make it more opaque.

Spattered effect Add all-over colour to a placemat by spattering it with specks of paint. First dilute the paint with a little water, then dip the tip of an artists' brush into it. Hold the brush over the fabric and tap it firmly against the handle of another artists' brush, or against your finger. It's a good idea to practise the technique on a piece of scrap paper first.

Fruit print Tablecloth

Create a delicious paint effect on fabric using cut fruit splashed with bright fabric paints. This is an ideal way to add zest to tablecloths, placemats and napkins.

Printing using fruit is a quick and novel way to decorate your tablelinen. Simply slice your chosen fruit in half, cover the cut surface with fabric paint and press it on to the fabric.

The example shown here and over the page is a bright summery tablecloth decorated with oranges, lemons and limes in fresh citrus colours. Most fruits can be used for this printing technique, providing they are firm and evenly shaped. Try starfruit covered in gold or silver paint, or stamp with apples in shades of red and green. You can even use cherries and strawberries to make your prints, if they are slightly under-ripe.

The cut fruit halves tend to lose their shape after repeated use, so you may need to use several pieces for one design. Make a few prints on a piece of scrap paper before working on the fabric, to check that the fruit makes an even pattern.

Fabric paints can be obtained from craft stores and artists' supply shops. The paint used here should be left to dry for 24 hours but doesn't need to be ironed to fix the dye. Always follow the manufacturer's instructions, as some fabric paints need to be pressed to "set" the colours.

Oranges, lemons and limes make a perfect pattern for a summer tablecloth. Paint each fruit motif with several colours to give depth to the design.

PRINTING WITH CITRUS FRUIT

MATERIALS

Selection of oranges, lemons and limes

Sharp knife

Absorbent cloth (optional)

Old blanket, towel or sheet

Plain tablecloth

Pins

Masking tape

Fabric paints, in various colours

2 artists' brushes, one narrow

Scrap paper

1 Cut the fruit in half, slicing the lemons and limes lengthways. If the fruit is juicy, leave it to dry out for two hours or rub the cut surface briskly with an absorbent cloth to remove any excess liquid before using it to print.

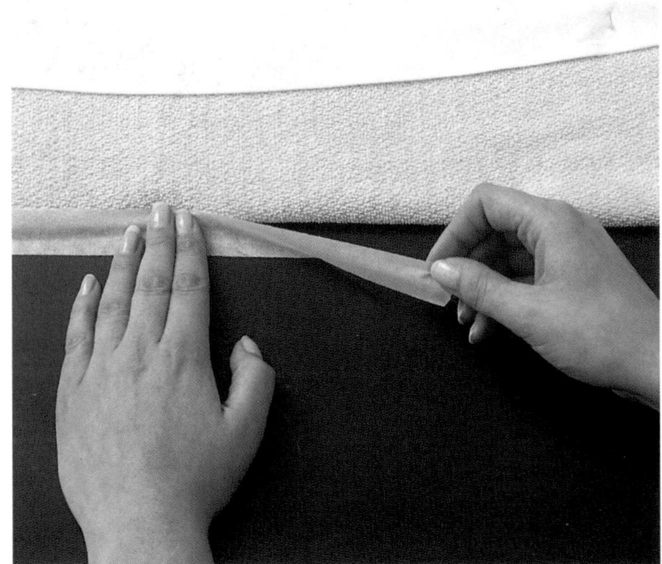

2 Fold an old blanket, towel or sheet in half and pin the tablecloth on top. Tape the edges of the blanket to your work surface to prevent it from moving when you are printing.

3 Use an artists' brush to apply the first paint colour to the cut flesh surface of an orange. The paints need to be applied thickly but not overloaded, or the colour will bleed into the cloth. Practise printing on a piece of scrap paper to check that the fruit is evenly covered.

4 Use a narrow artists' brush to apply the second paint colour around the cut edge of the rind and pith. Again, practise printing on scrap paper.

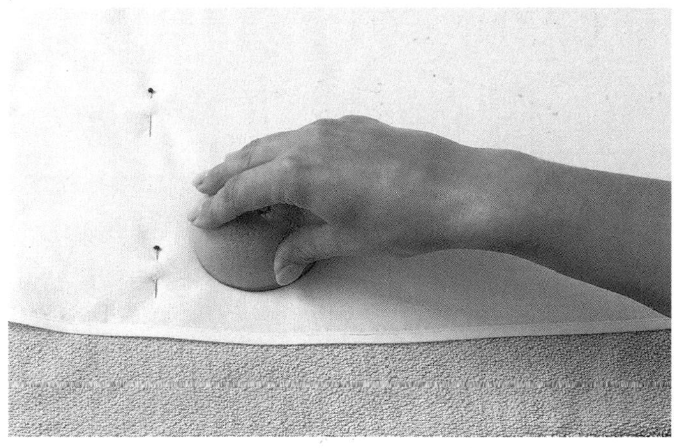

5 Starting 4cm ($1^{1}/_{2}$in) in from the edge of the tablecloth, place the orange, painted side down, on the fabric and press down firmly so that the paint transfers to the cloth.

6 Carefully lift the orange from the cloth, taking care not to move the fruit sideways as this will smudge the design.

7 If insufficient paint was transferred while pressing the fruit down, touch up the design with a paintbrush for a more defined shape and colour. Repeat steps 3-6 to print oranges all the way round the edge of the cloth, spacing them at regular intervals and touching up with a paintbrush as necessary.

8 Repeat steps 3-7 to print a row of lemons above the oranges, using additional or contrasting colours if desired. Then repeat to print a row of limes above the lemons. Leave to dry.

Bright painted citrus fruits, printed on a chequered napkin, make an attractive fabric design. Additional decoration, in the form of lightly brushed blue stripes, gives the napkin a bold decorative border.

DECORATING NAPKINS USING FRUIT WITH STALKS

Complete your table set by decorating napkins to match your cloth. The instructions below show how to print using fruit with stalks, such as apples and cherries. Arrange three fruit motifs, at angles, neatly in one corner of each napkin.

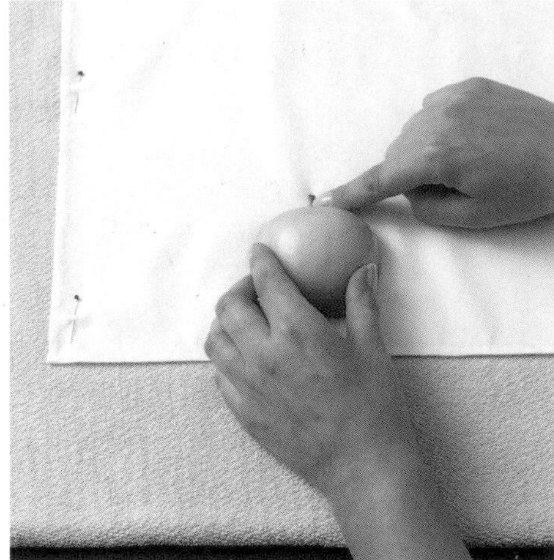

1 Prepare your fruit and napkins following steps 1-2 of PRINTING WITH CITRUS FRUIT, then apply your chosen paint colours as in steps 3-4, brushing paint along the stalk. Here, the skin and stalk, flesh and core of the apple were painted using three different colours.

2 Place the apple, painted side down, close to one corner of the napkin and press down firmly; use your free hand to press down on the stalk. Lift the apple away from the cloth, taking care not to move the fruit sideways. Touch up the design as necessary.

3 Repeat steps 1 and 2 above, using different paint colours, to print a further two apples to create a corner motif. Leave to dry.

Apples, printed squarely within the bold checks of this pretty fabric, create an effective fabric print. Use a grid, marked on the fabric with taylors' chalk, to help align your prints.

Soft white napkins randomly printed with large strawberries, are reminiscent of summer cream teas. Select very firm fruits, with leaves still attached for added interest.

Practical Placemats

Choose a set of smart placemats with neatly mitred borders to brighten up your breakfast or dining table. Choose washable fabrics in complementary or contrasting colours to suit the occasion.

Placemats are the perfect choice to add instant colour and interest to your table. Use them for informal dining such as breakfast, lunch or casual dinners, or place them on top of a long tablecloth in a coordinating or contrasting colour for a more formal look.

Placemats serve as a stage for your place settings. Choose contrasting colours and patterns to make your flatware stand out, such as sunny yellow woven mats under glossy plum-coloured plates, or pale green quilted mats under chunky raspberry red dishes. For a carefully coordinated look, choose placemats that echo the colours and patterns of your plates and glassware.

Placemats are readily available at home goods stores, department stores and linen outlets. They are usually quite inexpensive, so stock up on several different colours and textures. By simply swapping the place-mats, you'll be able to create a variety of different looks to suit your mood or the occasion.

Of course, if you are feeling inspired, you could make your own. There's an unlimited selection of materials to choose from – washable and shrinkproof fabrics are best to take the drama out of accident spills. Whether you are buying or making, a set of mats you can wash and press easily is a practical option.

▼ A simple printed fabric framed with a bold check produces a pair of placemats full of rustic charm. Add matching napkins for a perfectly coordinated finishing touch.

Placemats come in an endless array of colours, textures and patterns. You're sure to find a style that's just right for your table.

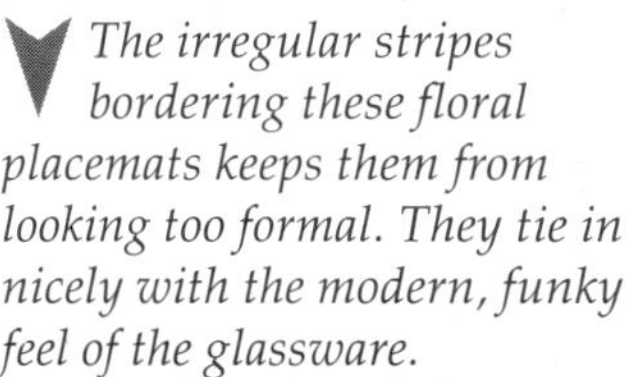

The irregular stripes bordering these floral placemats keeps them from looking too formal. They tie in nicely with the modern, funky feel of the glassware.

These Aztec-patterned placemats pull together the rustic feel of the plates, vase and serving dishes. Their bold colour gives a welcome lift to the browns of the pottery and table.

Pretty Paper Napkins

Add a flourish to your dining table with coloured and patterned napkins, twisted, folded and pleated into eyecatching shapes.

Paper napkins are a party and picnic staple, perfect for outdoor dining or children's celebrations. Available in a wide range of colours and designs, they can look surprisingly sophisticated. Select them to match your crockery or tablelinen, or to provide a splash of contrast colour.

Paper napkins can be folded or pleated in a host of clever ways, although classic origami folds are not especially effective because paper napkins don't crease easily. They will, however, twist into pretty shapes, and fold to create bread baskets and cutlery holders.

Paper napkins are available from stationers, supermarkets and specialist party shops, where you can have them specially printed for birthdays and anniversaries.

If you are using deep coloured napkins, try not to get them wet as the colour may run and stain clothes or tablelinen.

▲ ***Jacket required*** *Wrap your wine bottles in a napkin jacket to save your cloth from drips and stains. Fold a napkin in half diagonally, then fold down the pointed corners. Wrap it around the bottle, folded edge at the bottom, and tuck in the corners to secure.*

Five golden rings *If using napkin rings, add an individual detail with pleating. Open out the napkin and fold it back on itself to form a pleat in the desired width, then roll as usual to fit into the napkin ring. This ensures that any corner detailing is visible at both ends.*

Graceful glasses *Napkins in fresh summer colours look effective simply folded and placed in wine glasses. Match the colours in the napkins to your dinner service or table flowers for an inviting display.*

Bread winner *For an unusual side plate for bread, open out a napkin and fold each corner into the middle. Flip it over and repeat this process. Pull out the flap beneath each point to hold up the corners and form an instant basket.*

Pleated Table Napkins

Softly pleated napkins, coordinating with your crockery, tablecloth or a floral centrepiece, add the finishing touch to a sophisticated dining table.

For added flair at a dinner party or celebration meal, place an elegantly folded table napkin at each table setting – it will provide the perfect finishing touch.

There are lots of ways to fold napkins; the steps overleaf show you three different ideas, all based on the same principle of folding a napkin into accordion pleats: a wine-glass fan that adds height to the table, a butterfly fold that's tucked into a napkin ring in soft folds and a table-top fan that spans a place setting. Choose a style to suit your dinner table.

Experiment with different napkin folds for different occasions to vary the overall appearance of your table. With practice, you'll soon be able to fold napkins quickly and easily.

▲ *Pleated table napkins give a smart finish to formal table settings. Here, striking crimson napkins are folded into accordion pleats and arranged to fan out over the top of wine glasses. Starch the napkin if you want very crisp pleats (see the napkin on the left).*

BUTTERFLY FOLD NAPKIN

If you have napkin rings, fold your napkins into butterfly pleats for an elegant, low-key place setting. As the wrong side of the napkin is partly visible when fanned out on the table or plate, choose napkins that look good on both sides. Woven fabrics or printed fabrics where the print shows through clearly on the wrong side are ideal.

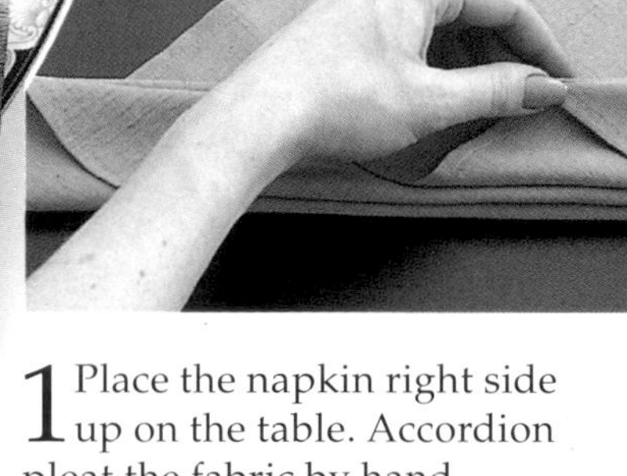

1 Place the napkin right side up on the table. Accordion pleat the fabric by hand, working diagonally from corner to corner.

2 Fold the napkin in half at the pleated centre. Holding the pleated centre, insert the napkin into a napkin ring, allowing both sides of the napkin to flair out.

WINE-GLASS FAN NAPKIN

Wine-glass fan napkins add height and a well-dressed finish to a special occasion dinner table. As the napkins are folded in half, this technique is suitable for napkins that are printed or finished on one side. If you have napkins with embroidered, shaped or trimmed edges, place the pleated napkin in the glass with the unfolded, decorative edge uppermost.

1 Fold the napkin in half, right side out, with the folded edge to your right. Accordion pleat by hand across the napkin, working away from you to the end of the napkin.

2 Place the napkin into a wine glass, folded edge uppermost, allowing the top of the napkin to fan out.

TABLE-TOP FAN NAPKIN

These table-top fan napkins are designed to sit just behind the table setting, or within it – spanning a decorative underplate, for example. You don't need napkins that are the same on both sides, but they should have a plain edge; this is because one half of the fan has a fold along the edge, while the other half reveals the hemmed napkin edges. For crisp pleats and to help the napkin stand up, starch the napkin before folding it.

1 Fold the napkin in half, right side out, with the folded edge to your left. Folding the first pleat down, accordion pleat across three-quarters of the napkin length.

2 Turn the napkin over so that the pleats are underneath, next to the table, and the unpleated section is to your right. Fold the top half of the napkin over the bottom half.

3 Hold the napkin upright, pinching the fold, so the open ends of the pleats point upwards.

4 Fold over the unpleated section of the napkin diagonally and tuck it into the back of the pleats to form a stand. Place on the table so the pleats fan out.

The neat curve of a table-top fan napkin adds height to a table setting, and suits both formal and informal styles. Avoid using lightweight napkins for this type of fold, and starch the napkin to ensure it stands upright.

Napkins folded into a wine-glass fan can be arranged in any style of glass or cup, provided the container is deep enough to hold the napkin in place. Here, a fanned napkin splays out over the sides of a spotted tumbler, adding a neat finishing touch to an informal table setting.

A plain white napkin made from fine cotton is displayed to advantage when arranged in butterfly folds, circled with a silver napkin ring. The fabric and embroidered edging look the same from both sides, making the napkin a perfect candidate for this type of fold.

FOLDED FLOWER NAPKINS

When you dress up your dining room for a really special occasion, the focus of the celebration will be the dining table. Elegantly folded napkins like these waterlily shapes, created using simple origami folds, lend an instant air of style and glamour to any table setting. Clever use of gold and silver in conjunction with decorated glassware and well thought-out lighting add to the atmosphere. Coordinate crisp cotton or linen napkins with your dining room decor for a sophisticated feel.

Use simple origami techniques to fold crisp cotton or linen napkins into multi-petalled flowers, which you can use to grace each place setting. For the best results, use quite large, square napkins which will make soft, full flowers.

1 FOLDING IN THE CORNERS
Press the napkin well and lay it flat on the table, with the wrong side up. Fold each corner into the centre to make a smaller square.

2 FOLDING THE CORNERS AGAIN
Fold the corners into the centre of the napkin a second time, creating an even smaller square. Turn the folded napkin over, and fold the corners in a third time, to make a smaller square; use your fingers to hold the folds down at the centre of the napkin as you work.

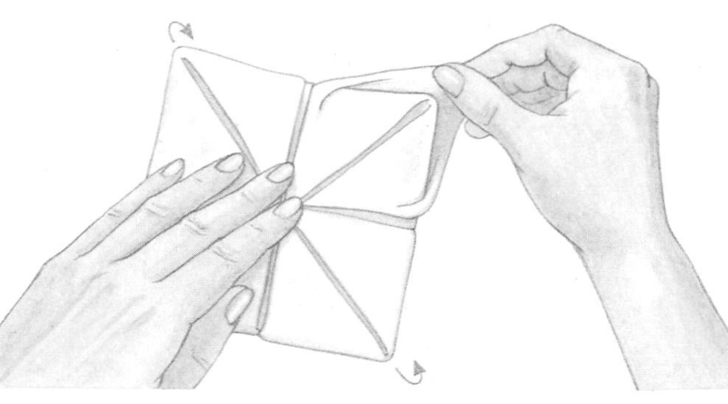

3 FORMING THE PETALS
Holding the centre folds in place with one hand, put your other hand behind the napkin and carefully draw one of the corners from the centre back outwards until it forms a peak, cupping the folded corner. Repeat at each corner to form four 'petals'.

4 FORMING THE SEPALS
Reach behind the flower, between the petals, and bring forward the corner flaps to form the sepals, as in step 3.

Folded Napkin Cutlery Holders

Dress your table in style by marking each place setting with a neatly folded napkin. For a clever yet practical touch, you can fold the napkins to double as cutlery holders.

You can fold napkins in numerous ways to create looks to suit any occasion. The napkins shown on the following pages are all designed to lay flat at a place setting – either on the table or a plate – and are folded to form a neat pocket to hold individual sets of cutlery. Quick and easy to fold, these napkins are perfect for dressing up a casual breakfast tray or for transforming a table for an impromptu dinner party.

There are three styles to choose from. The flipped-points fold produces a napkin with elegant points at the top and bottom. Alternatively, you can try your hand at the horizontal or diagonal fold designs; both form a rectangular holder, with either a simple horizontal or a double-striped diagonal pocket across the front for slotting in your cutlery.

The style, pattern and colour of the napkin you use determines the finished effect. Select bold checks or stripes in bright colours to add a cheerful touch to lunch or breakfast, or opt for dainty, lace-edged napkins for a romantic supper for two.

By selecting your napkin carefully, you can produce a dramatic result with just a few basic folds. Here, the blocks of rich colour and toning stripes of the napkin complement the bold fold lines of the cutlery holder's design.

FLIPPED-POINTS FOLD NAPKIN

A bright red napkin, neatly folded following the flipped-point technique, swiftly transforms an al fresco *lunch into a special occasion.*

1 Fold the napkin in half, right side facing outwards, the fold at the bottom. Fold it in half again, with the napkin corners at upper right. Fold back the first layer diagonally, bringing the corner down to the lower left.

2 Fold back the second layer of the napkin, so that the corner touches the centre fold of the first layer. Fold back the corner of the first layer from the lower left to meet the corner of the second layer at the centre fold.

Cutlery sits snugly inside the folded napkin, creating a neat, understated table setting.

3 Divide the napkin into thirds, then fold the thirds at each side under the centre third to finish (see left).

DIAGONAL FOLD NAPKIN

1 Fold the napkin in half, with the right side facing outwards and the fold at the bottom. Then fold the napkin in half again, with the corners of the napkin pointing towards the upper right.

➤ *A smart, individual set of cutlery slots neatly between the two diagonal bands of this napkin for a chic, sophisticated finish.*

2 Fold back the first layer of the napkin diagonally at the corner by about 5cm (2in).

3 Fold the same corner over itself twice more to create a diagonal band across the napkin, running from the top left corner to the bottom right corner.

4 Fold back the second layer of the napkin, tucking the corner underneath the diagonal band to create a second band about 2.5cm (1in) wide.

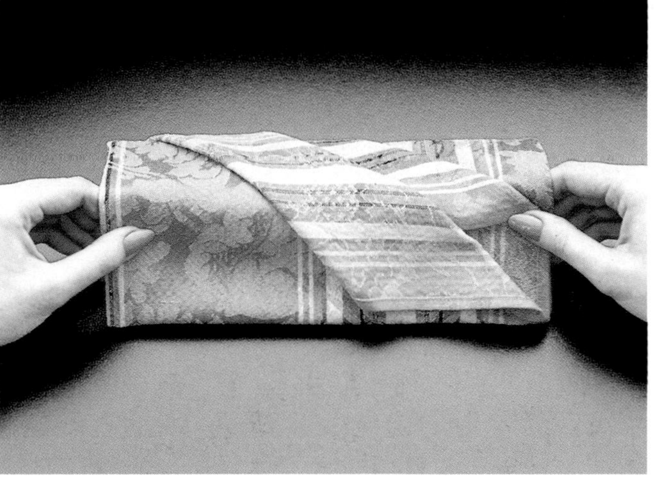

5 To finish, fold the top and bottom edges of the napkin to meet on the underside (see above).

HORIZONTAL FOLD NAPKIN

The delicate laced edge of this linen napkin softens the lines of the crisply pressed folds, adding a touch of femininity.

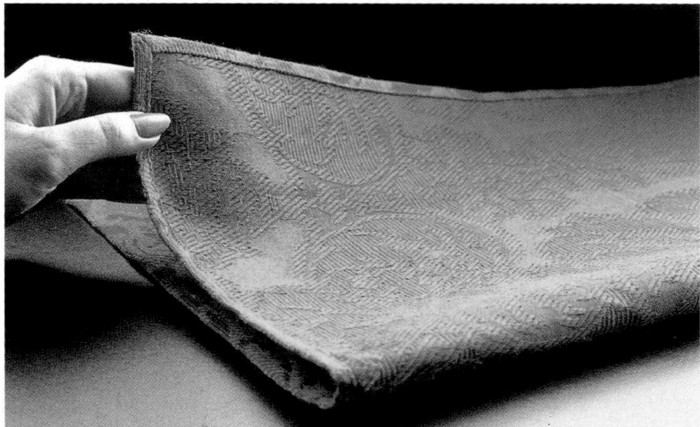

1 Fold the napkin in half, with the wrong side facing outwards and the fold at the bottom.

2 Fold back one third of the top layer of the napkin back to form a centre band.

If you prefer a more minimalist look, opt for the horizontal fold design. As both sides of the fabric are on show, a textured napkin in a plain colour is the perfect choice.

3 Holding the napkin at each end of the centre band, turn it over. Fold in the sides to meet at the centre back, then fold the napkin in half (see left).

Rosette Napkin Ties

Rosettes of fabrics gathered on to napkin ties add a festive twist to a plain table setting.

These inventive napkin ties lift any place setting out of the ordinary but all you need is some scraps of fabric to make them. Each rosette is artfully created by rolling a gathered strip of neatened fabric around a tie. The ties are then wrapped around the napkin to form a solid band about the centre or in a criss-cross pattern, depending which you prefer.

Choose a fairly crisp fabric which will hold the shape of the rosette. Crisp white cotton or cream linen is a classic choice but make sure that the linen is very fine; handkerchief linen is ideal. On linen or cotton the best way to finish the fabric edge is to press a very narrow turning to the wrong side, then zigzag with a narrow stitch over the edge from the right side.

Shiny shot organza is another good option for sparkly, festive rosettes. On organza and similar lightweight fabrics, a narrow zigzag stitch will roll the fabric edge as it stitches to make a fine and delicate finish without pressing the edge under. Using two toning shades or tints works well for these napkin ties. After neatening the edges, the two strips are gathered and finished as one fabric. Alternative colour options could combine red and green for a Christmas table; or navy blue with a deep plum for a subtle setting.

▲ *Choose between the sophisticated sheen of metallic shades of organza or the clean crispness of white or off-white linen that matches the napkin.*

Making linen rosettes

Rosette napkin ties made out of linen require half the fabric of organza ones but the method for making them up is much the same for each. Choose a colour that matches your napkins for understated elegance at the dinner table or opt for a contrasting shade of tie for a bolder effect.

MATERIALS

For each tie:

10cm (4in) of 90cm (36in) wide handkerchief linen

Matching thread

1 CUTTING OUT
Cut two rosette pieces 6.5 x 45cm (2½ x 18in). If the fabric has a good selvedge use this for the inside short edge. Cut one strip for tie 2.5 x 65cm (1 x 25½in).

2 STITCHING EDGES
Press 3mm (⅛in) to wrong sides along all raw edges of tassels. Zigzag stitch over pressed edges along long edges then short edges. Finish thread ends.

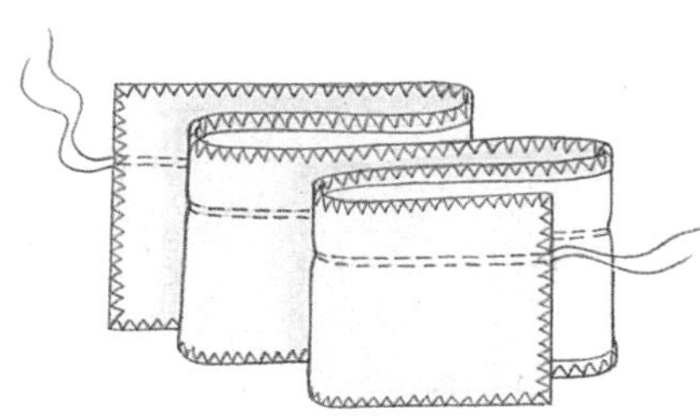

3 STITCHING GATHERS
Stitch a gathering stitch (longest machine stitch) along 2cm (¾in) in from one long edge. Stitch a second row 3mm (⅛in) above first.

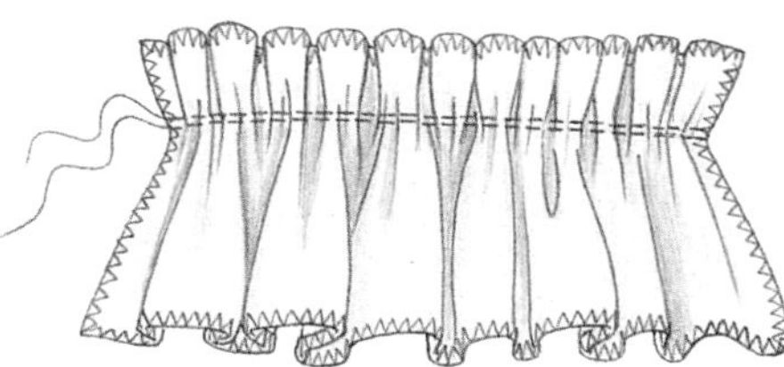

4 GATHERING TASSEL
Start pulling up gathers from each end. Secure gathering thread neatly at one end which will be on outer edge of rosette. Continue gathering from other end until it measures 15cm (6in) and secure threads.

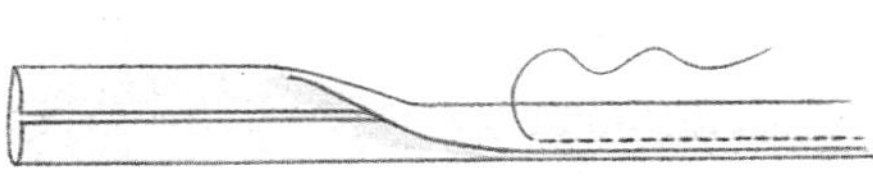

5 MAKING TIE
Press tie in half lengthways. Open out and press long raw edges in to meet at centre. Re-press in half and stitch long edges together.

The rose swirls are made by gathering the fabric at the base.

6 WRAPPING ROSETTE
Handstitch end of tie to inner edge of fabric. Then wrap fabric around and, using same thread, stitch through rosette level with gathering. Continue wrapping and stitching until rosette is complete. Stitch other rosette to other end of tie.

Organza rosettes

MATERIALS

For each tie:

10cm (4in) of 90cm (36in) wide organza in each of two toning colours

Toning thread

1 CUTTING OUT ORGANZA
Cut out in same way as linen example but cut two rosette pieces for each rosette, one from each fabric.

Two close shades of silver and pewter organza make shimmery duo-tone rosettes.

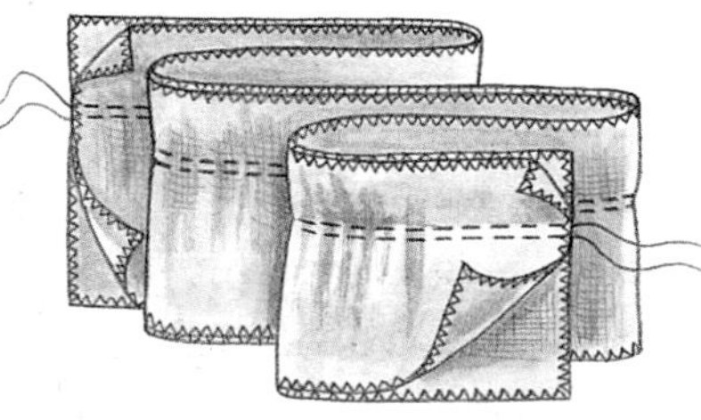

2 MAKING ORGANZA ROSETTE
Stitch around raw edge of rosette piece using a narrow zigzag stitch. This will naturally roll the fabric edge, giving a neat finish. Place one fabric layer on top of other and gather the two as one, as in step 3 above. Complete, as in steps 4-6 above.

Velvet Bow Napkin Rings

Deep hues of midnight velvet are perfect for these sophisticated napkin rings. Make them plain or add a glitter trim to the centre.

For our bows we used one colour velvet for the bow and covered ring, and a second colour for the bow-centre. If you are making a set of napkin rings you could choose three toning colours and intermix them within the bows. Alternatively, you could choose just two colours and add a glittery trim around the bow centre, or you could make the whole ring from a single colour.

The bow is made first, then attached to the ring with stitching at each side. For the ring, a section is cut from the cardboard roll from the centre of bathroom tissue. This is then covered with velvet to match the bow. The fabric can be stuck in place using either fabric glue or double-sided sticky tape.

The napkin rings with glitter trim are made in just the same way as those with the plain velvet bows. The only difference is that the glitter trim is wrapped around the centre before the bow is stitched to the ring.

Whether you want to have a romantic dinner for two or to impress a gathering of important guests, these softly folding bows in rich velvet will ensure that the table settings look good enough to eat.

Making napkin rings

The velvet bows are attached to cardboard rings covered with velvet to match the bows. The bows' centres are covered in a contrasting colour velvet.

Add party sparkle to the bow centres with a sequin waste trim.

MATERIALS

For each tie:

18 x 13cm (7 x 5⅛in) velvet for bow

5 x 15cm (2 x 6in) velvet to cover ring

9 x 7cm (3½ x 2¾in) velvet for bow-centre

Sewing thread

Cardboard from bathroom tissue roll

Fabric glue or double-sided adhesive tape

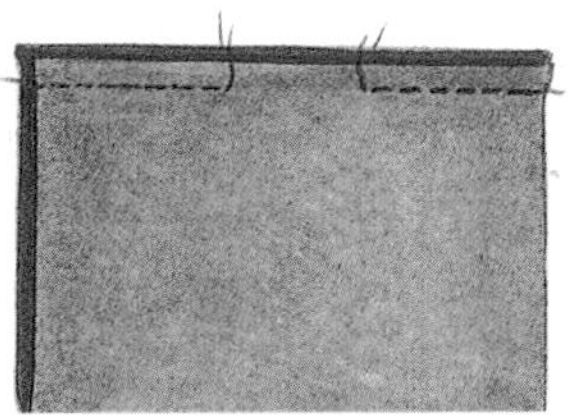

1 Stitching back seam With right sides facing, fold bow piece in half widthways and stitch the 13cm (5⅛in) long edges together, 1cm (⅜in) in from edges, leaving a 4cm (1½in) gap at the centre.

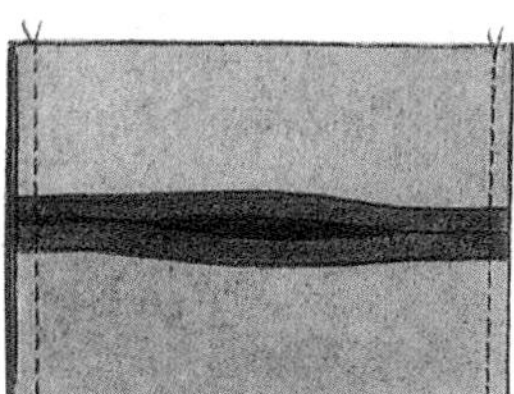

2 Stitching the ends Finger press seam open and arrange it at centre of piece. Pin; stitch across both short edges 1cm (⅜in) in from edges. Turn right side out. Use scissors or knitting needle to push out corners. Slipstitch opening closed.

3 Stitching bow-centre With right sides facing, fold bow in half lengthways and stitch the 9cm (3½in) edges together 1cm (⅜in) in from edges. Finger press seam open. Turn bow-centre right side out and arrange so the seam is at the centre of one side.

4 Pinning bow-centre With seam on bow at the back and seam on bow-centre facing inwards, pin one end to back of bow piece. Wrap centre around bow, pulling the bow in tightly.

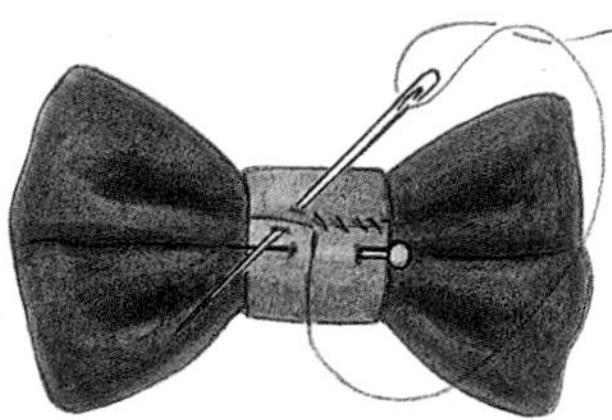

5 Stitching bow-centre With centre pulled tight, pin other end of centre over first end. Allowing an overlap, trim away any excess from ends of bow-centre. Handstitch end of bow-centre securely at back of bow.

6 Covering ring Cut a 2cm (¾in) wide ring from cardboard roll. Wrap velvet around. Allow for a 1cm (⅜in) overlap at end and trim off excess length. Apply glue or adhesive tape inside ring at one edge. Stick one edge of fabric in place, then apply glue or adhesive tape to the other inside edge and stick other edge in place.

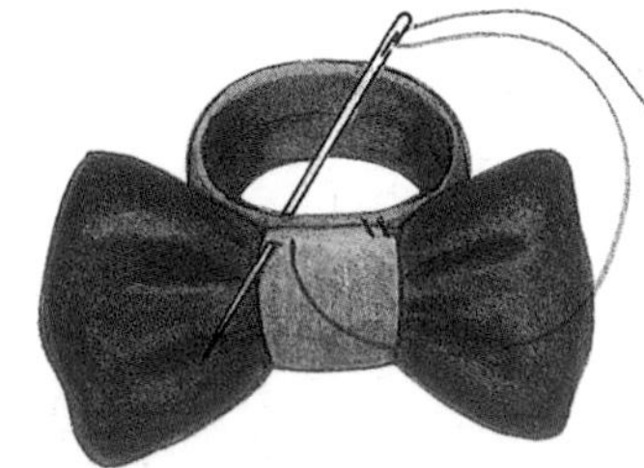

7 Stitching bow to ring Place bow to ring so it covers the overlapping fabric edges. Stitch the bow-centre to each edge of the ring each side and the centre of bow-centre as shown.

Adding glitter trims

MATERIALS

9cm (3½in) of 8.5cm (3⅜in) wide sequin waste

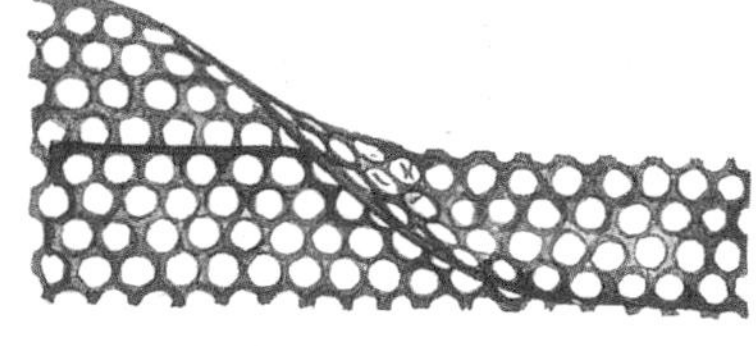

1 Folding sequin waste Make velvet bow and attach the bow-centre following the previous instructions, steps 1-5. Fold sequin waste in three lengthways as shown.

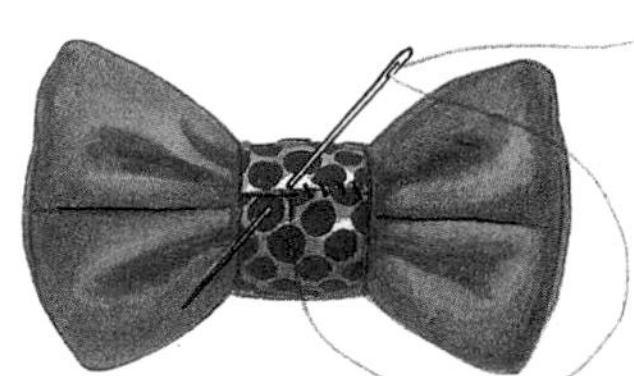

2 Attaching sequin waste Wrap the sequin waste around on top of the bow-centre and pin the overlapping ends at the back of the bow. Trim excess sequin waste and stitch the overlapping ends through the holes in the sequin waste. Complete the napkin ring following Making napkin rings, steps 6 and 7.

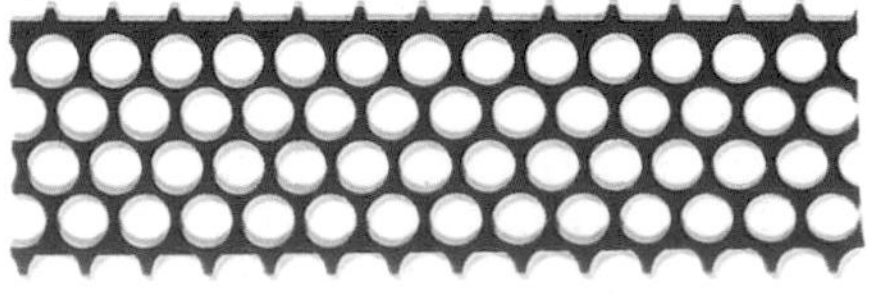

This shiny punched material is what is left when sequins are made; it is available from craft or fabric stores.

Fruit Napkin Rings

Brighten up summer mealtimes and picnics with these charming fruit napkin rings. The fruits are hand moulded from papier mâché pulp, which gives them a realistic, textured finish; then they're painted in bright, glossy colours.

Whet your guests' appetites for a really scrumptious dinner with these mouthwatering fruit napkin rings painted in realistic colours.

Painting the Fruits

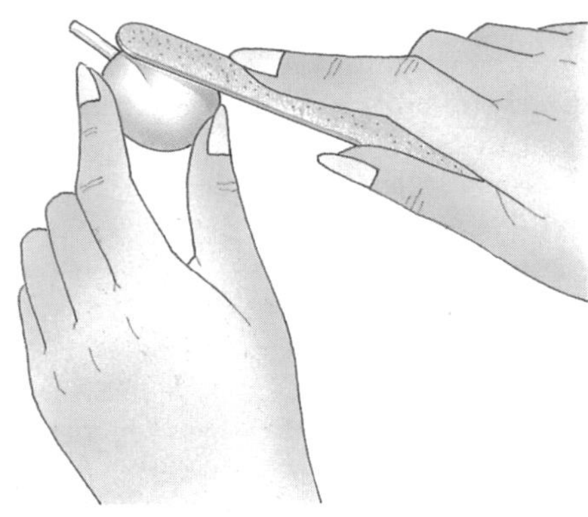

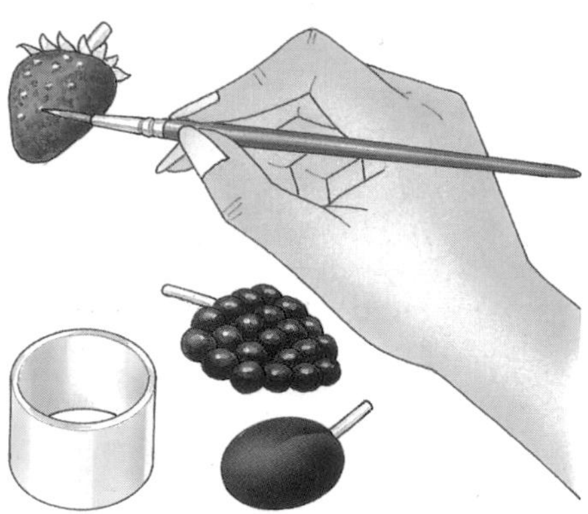

1 APPLYING THE UNDERCOAT
Sand the plum with the nail file to smooth the surface. Paint the fruits, leaves and napkin rings with a coat of white emulsion (latex) or gesso and leave them to dry.

2 STARTING THE PAINTING
Paint the napkin rings gold and the plum and grapes purple. Paint the strawberry red. When the strawberry is dry, use the tip of the fine artists' brush to paint on tiny yellow dots, to represent pips.

3 PAINTING THE OTHER FRUITS
Paint the lemon yellow and leave it to dry. Lighten the yellow paint with a little white, and use this to highlight the top of the lemon. In another saucer, mix yellow with red to make orange, and use this to paint the orange. Add a little brown to the remaining orange paint, and use this to paint the pineapple.

4 ADDING THE DETAILS
Paint the orange and grape stalks brown. Paint the plum stalk, pineapple leaves, orange leaf and lemon leaf green. In a saucer, mix a tiny dab of black into green to make dark green, and use this to paint the vine leaf and the strawberry stalk and sepal. Leave the paint to dry.

5 FINISHING OFF
Using PVA adhesive and taking the pictures as a guide, glue the fruits and leaves on to the napkin rings. Leave the glue to set.

Leafy Touches

Swirling stems of glossy ivy or fragrant honeysuckle, posies of delicate freesias, clusters of aromatic herbs or large, single leaves – wrap them around simple napkins to make beautiful table decorations in an instant.

Wrap small-leaved ivy around a white napkin. The combination of green leaves and white linen gives a stylish look to any table setting.

Trailing stems or clusters of leaves and flowers create instant napkin decorations and give any table setting an extra special touch.

The garden, grocery store or florist can all be raided for plants to twine around napkins, creating a delightful alternative to ordinary napkin rings. Creeping or climbing plants are ideal because they are so easy to wrap around a napkin. Alternatively, twist the napkin into a loose knot, and tuck a few flowers or leafy stems inside.

This ivy-leaved napkin ring is quick to make from a single stem of ivy twisted loosely around a neatly folded napkin. If you haven't got any ivy in your garden, you could do the same thing with artifical leaves.

HERB RING

Clusters of freshly picked herbs, from the garden, patio, window box or even the supermarket, garnish a striped linen napkin.

MATERIALS

Fresh herbs

Raffia

Napkin

Scissors

1 PREPARING THE NAPKIN
Pleat the napkin and tie a wide piece of raffia around it. Finish with a knot on top and cut off the raffia ends, leaving about 7.5cm (3in) on either side. Fan the napkin out to form soft, but definite, pleats.

2 TYING ON THE HERBS
Gather a selection of herbs into a small bunch. Put flat-leaved herbs, like bay or French parsley, at the back of the bunch, so that the bunch will lie flat on the napkin. Tie the herbs with a little more raffia and lay them on top of the napkin.

FREESIA POSY

Add a waft of perfume to the table with deliciously scented freesias slipped into a pleated napkin ring.

To make the napkin ring, pleat up a length of satin ribbon in your chosen colour, stitching it down the centre in a matching thread, and joining the ends at the back. Slip the napkin inside the ribbon ring, fanning out the edges. Then add a few flowers in a matching shade.

GRASS RING

A really simple napkin tie can be created from a bunch of long bear grass, twisted into a knot round the napkin. Make sure the grass is clean – wash it before you start, drying it by rolling it in a tea towel.

Roll the napkin along its length and let it unravel slightly into loose folds.

Cut the grass into equal lengths and arrange it so that it all lines up at the bottom. Tie the grass around the napkin in a simple knot, ensuring that the grass fans out at the top end for a natural effect.

HONEYSUCKLE TWIST

Mix the summer colours of honeysuckle with a golden yellow napkin. Twisting the napkin into a simple knot takes no time at all, yet looks really artistic.

MATERIALS

Honeysuckle

Large yellow napkin

MAKING THE TWIST

1 FOLDING THE NAPKIN
Place the napkin in front of you diagonally, so that it forms a diamond shape. Fold the top point down to the centre and the bottom point up, so that it just overlaps the first.

2 FORMING A STRIP
Fold the top and bottom edges over again so that the napkin forms a long strip.

3 MAKING THE KNOT
Fold the ends of the napkin to the centre, twisting them into a knot.

4 ADDING HONEYSUCKLE
Ease the knot open and slide two or three short stems of honeysuckle inside, passing them right the way through. Arrange them for the most pleasing effect.

This bright yellow napkin is knotted with stems of honeysuckle. Other trailing stems of flowers can work just as well: try jasmine, Virginia creeper or hops.

LEAF TIE

To make this simple tie, cut a single gladiola leaf and a single flower on a short stalk. Soak the leaf for about an hour in warm water to soften it, then dry it thoroughly.

Wrap the leaf around the folded napkin, then trim off the ends at an angle. To finish, slip the flower into the leaf circle, trimming the stalk so that it doesn't show.

Table Decorations

Enhance a special occasion table setting with fresh flower and foliage napkin rings, menu cards and place cards and candlesticks. All the flower trims are simple and inexpensive to create, using sticky tape and a little florists' wire.

Stand a fat candle in a hurricane lamp, and scatter fresh flower petals around it, for a sweet-scented and summery table centrepiece.

Gold plate *Team dainty violet Trachelium with bright yellow/gold Rudbeckia, or cone flower, for a beautiful summer look. Choose a contrasting shallow plate for the blooms or use a large serving plate from your dinner service. The subtle, batik-style tablecloth serves to emphasize the exotic feel.*

Pottery centrepiece *To create a modern, ethnic look, choose an understated, unpainted pottery bowl for your centrepiece. Place a few palm leaves and different types of grasses, tied with long supple leaves, inside. Add a loose bunch of lilac Scabious in a small clay flower pot to give the table arrangement some extra height.*

Pretty pinks *Make a seasonal setting with selected flowers from your garden. These delightful pink Lavatera and Calendula are in contrast to the stylish blue and black dish and blue and white table cloth. With just a few flowers and in a very short time a stunning table centrepiece has been created.*

Clever Carnations

Carnations are inexpensive, colourful and readily available all year round. Pick up a bunch at the supermarket for a last-minute centrepiece – with a little imagination, you can create an eyecatching arrangement.

Curving stems of grey-green eucalyptus are the perfect complement to a fresh bunch of ruby red carnations. A simple white jug sets them off.

Naturally long-lasting, carnations can bloom for up to three weeks in the home. This means you can buy them well ahead of time so you don't have to worry about creating a floral centrepiece on the night of your party or dinner. However, if you're putting together an impromptu dinner or need a last-minute arrangement, you can create a variety of stunning centrepieces with the carnations that are readily available at your local supermarket or convenience store.

For a simple arrangement, fill a classic container such as a plain vase or jug with carnations. Carnations always mix well with foliage, so buy a few stems or pick some from your garden or patio. Asparagus fern is a popular complement to carnations, but you can use almost any leafy plant you like.

Shorter stems look good set at different heights in a range of smaller containers, like matching glasses or jars of varying sizes. Full blooms look pretty inserted into a hanging foam ball. Alternatively, create a carnation "gateau", adding in sprigs of baby's breath or gypsophila.

CARNATION GATEAU

Turn full-blown carnations into an ingenious arrangement, perfect for a buffet table or sideboard. Make sure you use floral foam designed especially for fresh flowers: it's usually bright green.

MATERIALS

Carnations

Round piece of floral foam

Gypsophila (baby's breath)

Moss

Cake stand

1 STARTING THE DISPLAY
Soak the foam well and place it on the cake stand. Cut down the stems of the carnations to about 5-7.5cm (2-3in) and push them into the foam. Work around the bottom edge of the foam first, then fill in the top.

2 COMPLETING THE DISPLAY
Cut small sprigs of gypsophila and push these in among the carnations. Cover any visible foam with pieces of moss.

This pretty pink centrepiece looks formal enough for a dinner party or old-fashioned tea party – and it can be put together in minutes.

CONDITIONING FLOWERS

Carnations will last much longer if you condition them. First trim the bottom of the stems diagonally and strip off the lower leaves. Then put the carnations in a large jug or bucket of deep, cool water and leave them for a couple of hours in a cool, shady room.

When you are ready to arrange the flowers, add some conditioner to the vase.

For a simpler, more contemporary look, choose brightly coloured carnations and original containers, like the blue drinking glasses here.

HOME-MADE CONDITIONER

Make your own flower conditioner by mixing one part lemonade to two parts water, and arrange your carnations in this. Add a dash of bleach to kill off any harmful bacteria.

Shaped Arrangements

Use florists' foam to create shaped flower arrangements to use as decorations or for table centrepieces. You can buy a ready-shaped foam ring, or cut your own design – choose from the heart, star, horseshoe or clover featured here.

A ready-cut florists' foam ring provides a shapely base for this floral display of Ranunculus, anemones and mimosa, over a frill of eucalyptus leaves.

HEART OF FLOWERS

This pink, heart-shaped arrangement can be used to decorate a celebratory table for an anniversary or a romantic Valentine's day dinner. You can alter the choice of flowers to create an alternative colour theme or to fit the season. The pretty pink of this arrangement is created predominantly with daisies and bergenias, teamed with half a dozen roses for a luxurious touch. You need only buy short-stemmed flowers for the display, as you will be trimming them down.

Place the finished arrangement on a solid base – a decorative tray or plate is ideal for a table centrepiece.

The completed arrangement is about 20cm (8in) wide.

TEMPLATES
One square = 2cm (¾in)

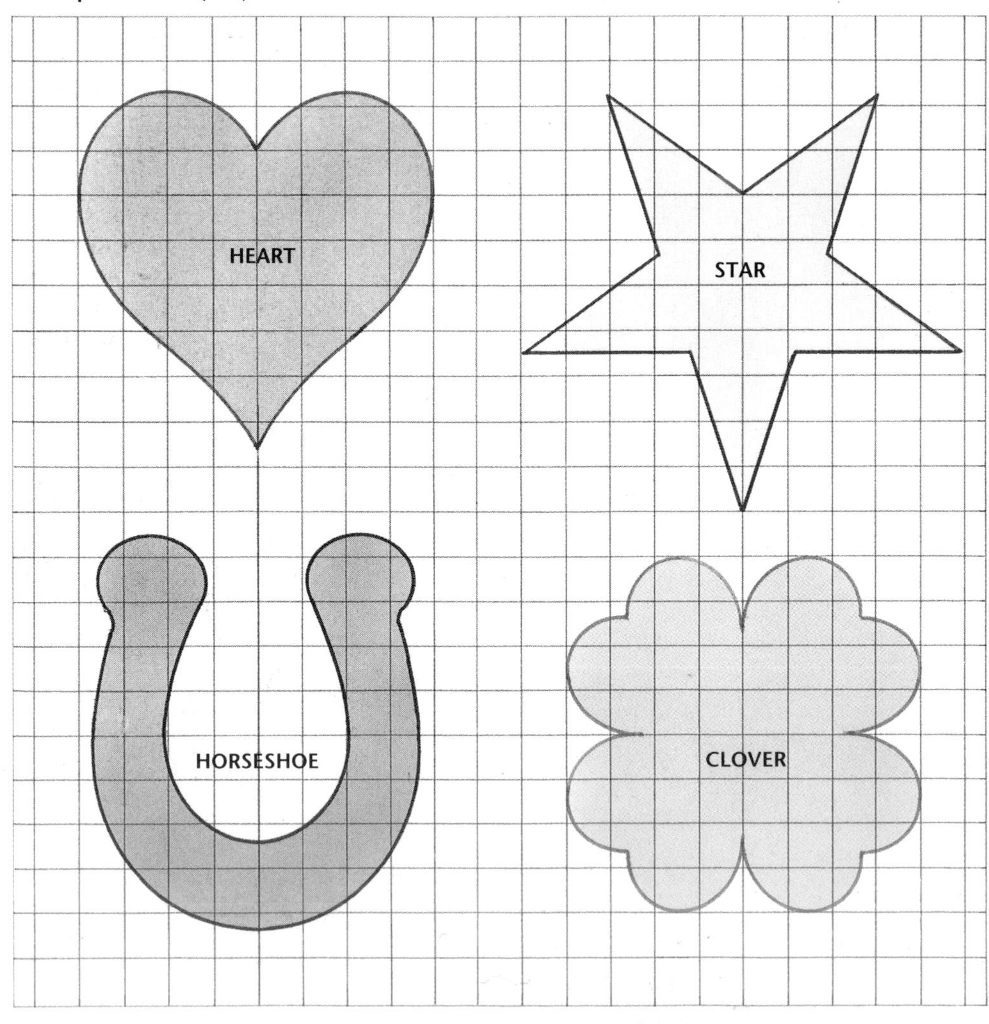

MATERIALS

Flowers for the arrangement: bellis, buttercups, small roses, bergenias, ageratums, violets, small white wax flowers and ivy sprigs

Block of florists' foam

Tracing paper and pencil

Ruler

Paper

Sharp knife

Wooden skewers in a variety of lengths

Scissors and pins

Fine knitting needle

Bowl

Flat plate

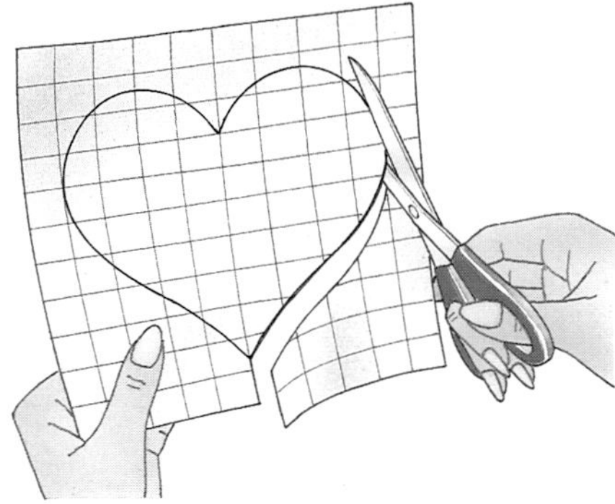

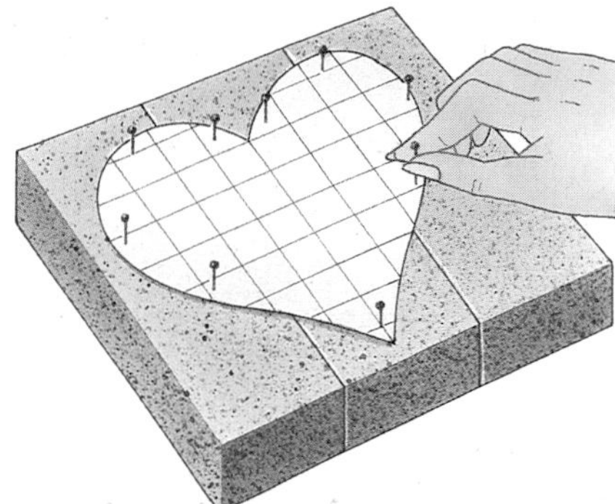

1 PREPARING THE TEMPLATE
Enlarge the heart template using the grid or a photocopier: each square on the grid represents 2cm (¾in). Trace the heart on to paper and cut it out.

2 PREPARING THE FOAM
Soak the florists' foam in a bowl of water until it is damp. Using the sharp knife, cut the block into long sections about 3cm (1¼in) thick.

3 PINNING ON THE TEMPLATE
Arrange the sections of florists' foam into a flat block, large enough for the heart template to fit on top. Pin the template in place on top of the foam.

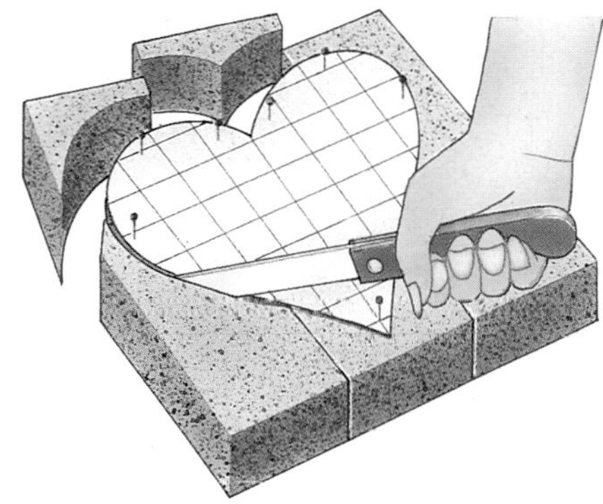

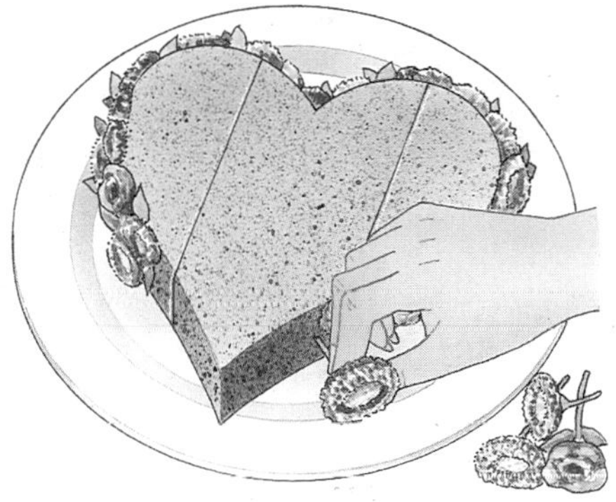

4 CUTTING THE HEART
Using the sharp knife and following the heart template outline, cut through the florists' foam, gradually slicing away to form the heart shape. Carefully remove the paper and pins, taking care not to crumble the oasis.

5 SECURING THE HEART
To hold the blocks of florists' foam together, poke skewers through the heart shape from one side to the other. Put the heart shape into a shallow bowl of water until the oasis is thoroughly damp.

6 ADDING THE FLOWERS
Sit the heart on a flat plate. Trim the flower stems to 2.5cm (1in) and keep them in water while you arrange them. Starting at the side edges, carefully stick the flower stems into the foam, packing the flowers densely together. If any flower stems are very delicate, make a hole in the oasis with a fine knitting needle first to avoid damaging the stem.

7 COMPLETING THE HEART
Working from the outside to the centre, cover the whole heart with flowers. Insert sprigs of ivy into any gaps. Display the heart on a plate or tray. Alternatively, use the template to cut out a heart from cardboard and cover it with silver foil, then stand the heart on top.

INSTANT DISPLAY

If you're short of time, use a ready-shaped ring of florists' foam as the base for your display, as shown in the picture on the opening page. You can buy these from florists' shops and craft stores. Soak the foam in water, then cover it with flowers as for the HEART OF FLOWERS, steps 6-7.

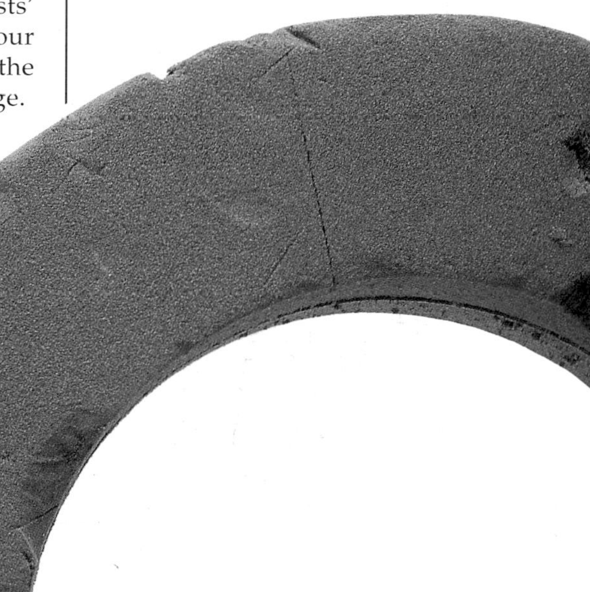

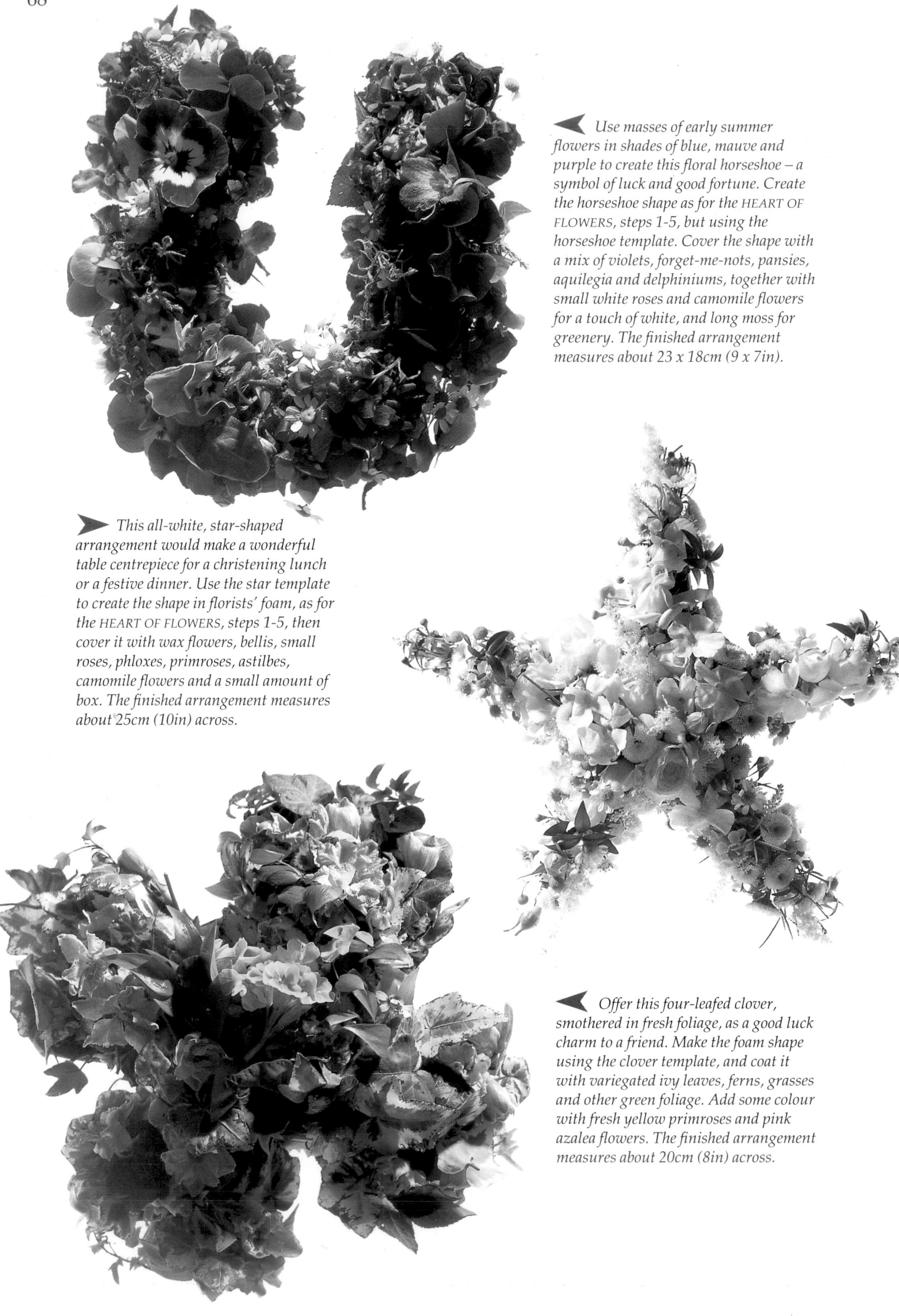

Use masses of early summer flowers in shades of blue, mauve and purple to create this floral horseshoe – a symbol of luck and good fortune. Create the horseshoe shape as for the HEART OF FLOWERS*, steps 1-5, but using the horseshoe template. Cover the shape with a mix of violets, forget-me-nots, pansies, aquilegia and delphiniums, together with small white roses and camomile flowers for a touch of white, and long moss for greenery. The finished arrangement measures about 23 x 18cm (9 x 7in).*

This all-white, star-shaped arrangement would make a wonderful table centrepiece for a christening lunch or a festive dinner. Use the star template to create the shape in florists' foam, as for the HEART OF FLOWERS*, steps 1-5, then cover it with wax flowers, bellis, small roses, phloxes, primroses, astilbes, camomile flowers and a small amount of box. The finished arrangement measures about 25cm (10in) across.*

Offer this four-leafed clover, smothered in fresh foliage, as a good luck charm to a friend. Make the foam shape using the clover template, and coat it with variegated ivy leaves, ferns, grasses and other green foliage. Add some colour with fresh yellow primroses and pink azalea flowers. The finished arrangement measures about 20cm (8in) across.

Pastel Party Piece

This pretty table centrepiece is ideal for a special lunch or supper, yet you can make it in just a few minutes. The soft pink and white blooms are arranged in blocks of colour in a shallow, circular design which looks attractive from all sides.

Recreate this pretty table arrangement in pink and white, or choose different seasonal flowers or colours to suit your own special occasion.

TABLE CENTREPIECE

Arranging flowers in blocks of colour in a circular bowl is a simple way to create a really successful display for a formal dining table, a buffet or even a small side table. Use two or three colours at most: try pink and white or blue, mauve and white, or pink, yellow and white. Keep the stems short and place the flowers close together.

MATERIALS

Large shallow glass or china bowl

Pink tulips, white tulips, pink Ranunculus, pink hyacinths, and white and pink spray chrysanthemums

Narrow mesh wire netting

Scissors

1 SHAPING THE FRAME
Pour a little water into the bowl. Crumple up the wire netting and fit it into the bowl. Lay out the flowers and, using the scissors, trim all the stems to about 10cm (4in) long.

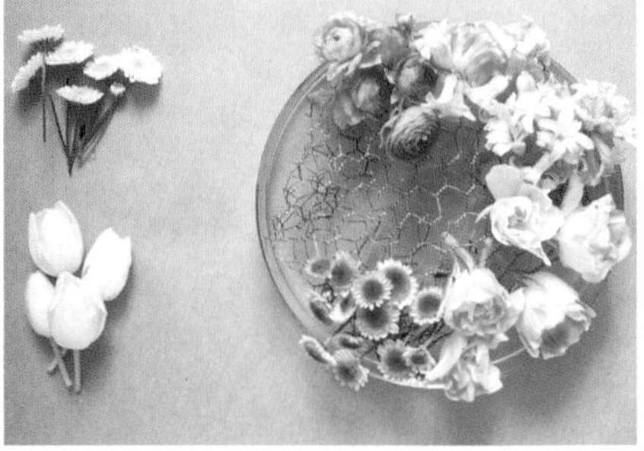

2 ARRANGING THE TULIPS
Starting at the outer edge, slot the stems of the pink tulips into the wire mesh to create a block of pink: arrange the flowerheads so that they face away from the centre of the bowl.

3 ADDING THE HYACINTHS
Arrange the pink hyacinth heads next to the pink tulips, making sure they cover as much of the wire mesh as possible.

4 ADDING MORE FLOWERS
Arrange a block of pink Ranunculus next to the hyacinths, and a block of pink spray chrysanthemums next to the pink tulips.

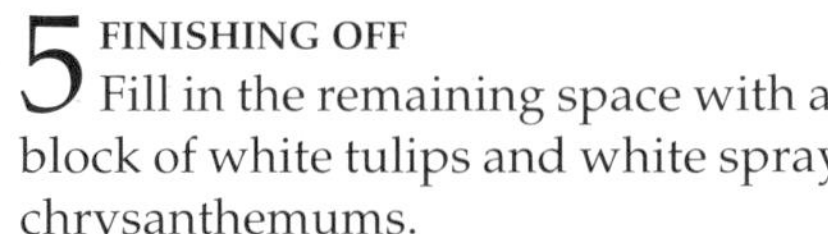

5 FINISHING OFF
Fill in the remaining space with a block of white tulips and white spray chrysanthemums.

▲ *This dainty three-colour summer arrangement would look pretty for a Sunday brunch or summer party. To copy this look, fill a small bowl with fragrant sweet peas, daisies and yellow button chrysanthemums.*

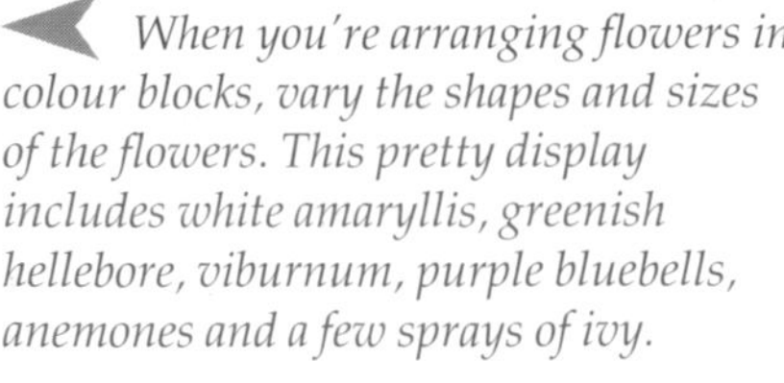

◀ *When you're arranging flowers in colour blocks, vary the shapes and sizes of the flowers. This pretty display includes white amaryllis, greenish hellebore, viburnum, purple bluebells, anemones and a few sprays of ivy.*

Tea Party

Fill teapots with flowers or potted plants for a pretty, witty display. Use just one or group several together – it's a great way to make the most of teapots that don't pour properly, and ones with broken handles, missing lids, cracks or chips.

A profusion of old-fashioned, full-blown pink and white roses fills a pretty china teapot, setting off the teapot's lovely floral design.

Flowers and plants go well in teapots, and the teapot needn't be perfect. You'll find plenty of cheap but appealing teapots that have seen better days in flea markets or garage sales. Small cracks can be repaired by smearing the inside surface with multi-purpose glue. This should seal the pot well enough to take water, but to make sure, you can put another container inside the teapot to hold the water – a jam jar or small yogurt container would work well.

Cut flower displays

To achieve a good balance, make sure the flowers are at least twice the height of the teapot. The teapot's narrow neck will support the flower stems so you won't need to use florists' foam or chicken wire.

Plants in teapots

To create a pretty accent for a house-warming party, place flowering houseplants still in their plastic pots inside a collection of teapots. After the party, the plants can be given as gifts to the new home owners.

Tulips have a tendency to droop, but these double tulips are well supported by their teapot container.

Three teapots in varying sizes – but all in shades of blue – make an attractive group using little potted primulas and a geranium.

An old silver-plated teapot needs only a few full-blown roses to create a romantic display.

DISPLAYS IN CUPS

For a pretty flower display on a small scale, pop a posy of blooms into a dainty china cup or mug. A small bunch in a teacup will brighten up a breakfast tray, and a group of flower-filled cups will create a fresh table centrepiece.

Yellow and blue spring flowers – hyacinths, primroses, grape hyacinths and narcissi – echo the colours and designs of their china containers.

TEA-TIME TREATS

Add instant charm to a kitchen table, tea-table or breakfast tray with a cluster of blooms spilling out from a teacup. Use flowers with open faces, such as roses, marigolds, cornflowers, Ranunculus, daisies, anemones, primroses and pansies. A densely bunched display looks best, so be generous with the flowers. For displays in teacups, cut each stem to the depth of the cup; for tall mugs, vary the height of the stems.

Choose cups or mugs which echo the flowers' colours or which create a striking contrast. Display the blooms in cups painted with floral designs to emphasize the theme. Place bold, bright flowers in chunky mugs with big floral motifs, and fragile blossoms in fine porcelain teacups with daintier designs. Scour flea markets and second-hand shops for elegant china cups. It doesn't matter if the rims are chipped – the flowers will disguise this as they spill over the edge of the cup.

A cluster of richly coloured pansies looks charming spilling out of this dainty china teacup, adding a jolly touch to the al fresco *tea-time setting. The cup and matching saucer are painted with pansies, so they are an especially apt choice.*

Mass bright flowers together in plain, shallow cups to create a decorative table centrepiece. Vivid orange Ranunculus and yellow roses are set off by starry, white spray chrysanthemums and clusters of wild carrot.

Pink pyrethrums, a white shasta daisy and a spray of delphiniums fill this sunny yellow teacup.

Upright pink campion flowers are softened by a cluster of white stars of Bethlehem. This exquisite display would make a charming addition to a breakfast tray.

Seasonal Berries

Use colourful ornamental berries for long-lasting, vibrant arrangements. Gather them for festive table decorations and unusual posies, or display bunches of glossy fruit-laden branches in naturally rugged containers.

Textured bark strips tied around a water-holding container set off this sculptural display of holly leaves, berries and crab apples.

Holly berries are a familiar and much-loved favourite for Christmas decorations, but there are many other berry bearing shrubs and hedgerow plants that you can cut and display indoors.

Pyracantha and cotoneaster bear red and orange berrries, and skimmia japonica has bright red berries lapped by rich green, aromatic leaves. Hypericum branches laden with oval berries are a popular addition to flower arrangements. Sweet briar, hawthorn and thorn bushes and rowan trees all bear crimson berries. For a contrast of shape and form use cherry-like crab apples and rosehips.

It is best to avoid using poisonous berries, such as yew and euonymus, if the displays are likely to be within the reach of children or pets.

For a warm glow, circle the rim and base of a hurricane lamp with dense clusters of ruby red cotoneaster berries. Using florists' wire, bind the berries into bunches, then attach the bunches to circlets of thick garden wire. When in place, make sure the berries from the top circlet do not dangle too close to the candle flame and be careful not to let the candle burn right down – this may cause the glass shade to shatter.

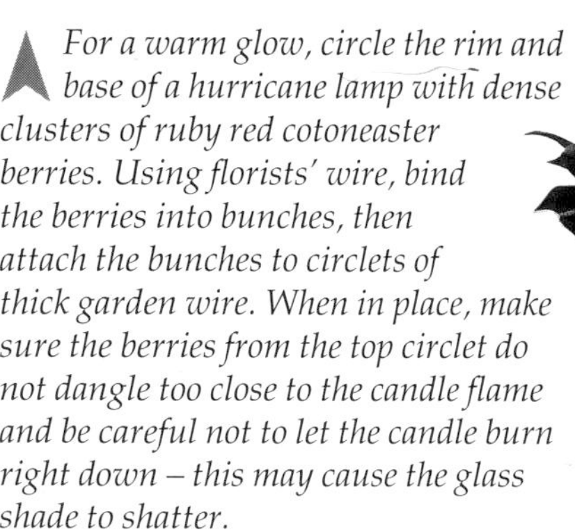

Use any non-poisonous berries for a simple table decoration, washing and drying the berries thoroughly beforehand. Try this idea for a festive table setting, decorating each of your guests' plates in the same way.

This "lollipop" arrangement is easy to make. Wire bunches of cotoneaster and sweet briar hips and wrap them with crisp white paper doilies to make posies. Insert the wires into a polystrene craft ball attached to a trimmed branch and display the arrangement in a terracotta or gleaming metal pot trimmed with more berries.

TUTTI FRUTTI

Concoct an exotic combination of flowers and fruits for a dazzling display, perfect for any special occasion. Organized into elaborate garlands or just piled into a dish, you'll be surprised how easy these displays are to assemble.

This quick and easy display uses yellow roses and winter jasmine set amongst tangerines and kumquats. Shiny leaves balance the bright colours.

fruit knife

grooving tool melon baller small biscuit cutters

Turning a simple dessert into a stunning creation is a lot easier than it looks. All of the ideas shown here can be achieved using a few basic techniques and the minimum of equipment.

Choosing Fruit

Melons make the best bowls for fruit salads and family sized containers for ice cream and sorbet. Use ogen, honeydew, cantaloup (rock) and watermelons. Make sure the melons are firm and unblemished. They should smell faintly sweet and should give slightly when pressed at the stalk end if they are ripe. Use oranges as individual containers.

Carving a Watermelon

Dazzle friends and family with a beautifully hand-carved watermelon (see page 81), filled with a simple selection of fruits. Here, the contents of the watermelon have been chopped and combined with one other variety of melon. Mint leaves provide the garnish. It's a salad that smacks of sun-drenched holidays.

MATERIALS

Tracing paper
Pen or pencil
Watermelon
Wooden skewer
Grooved citrus cutter

Trace this pattern and transfer it on to the watermelon; or design your own pattern.

1 Using a pen or pencil, trace your design on to a sheet of tracing or greaseproof paper. Place the tracing on the watermelon and, with a pointed wooden skewer, prick the outline of the design so that it appears on the watermelon.

2 Take a grooved citrus cutter and work around the marked outline. Repeat until the whole watermelon is carved. Cut off the top of the melon about a third of the way down and scoop out contents.

SWEETHEART SALAD

The cut-outs and shaping of this cantaloup (rock) melon are simple enough to carry a more varied selection of fruit. Choose a combination of colours, tastes and textures.

MATERIALS

Cantaloup melon
Small biscuit cutters
Sharp knife
Strawberries
Raspberries
Persimmons
Sprig of mint
Melon baller

1 Cut off the top of the melon and use a melon baller to scoop out the flesh. Use a rotating wrist action to achieve perfectly round balls. Refrigerate the balls until ready for use. Use a spoon to remove the pips and any remaining flesh.

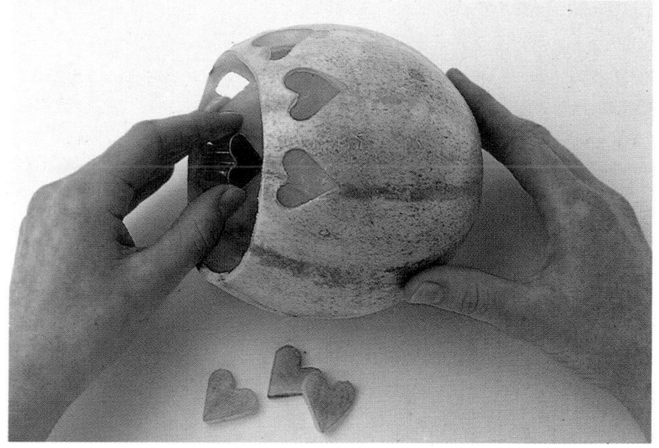

2 Rest the empty melon on its side. Work around the melon, stamping out shapes using a 2.5cm (1in) biscuit cutter. The row of hearts, or your preferred shape, should be approximately 2cm (3/4in) down from the top edge.

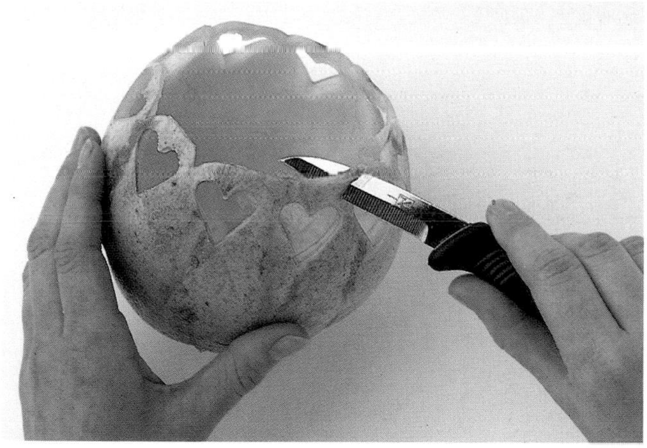

3 Take a very sharp knife and shape the top edge of the melon into scallops. Do this by cutting a small V into the edge, between each heart. Wash and prepare the rest of the fruit, combine with the melon balls and pile into the melon. Decorate with mint.

CARVED CITRUS CONTAINERS

Oranges are the perfect size and colour for turning into individual carved containers for sorbet or ice cream. Pink grapefruit can also be used as the colour of the skin is strong enough to show off the carved grooves to best effect.

Limes are very pretty when given this treatment, but bear in mind that you will need at least two for each person to ensure enough dessert! Limes and lemons do, however, make ideal containers if you intend to serve sorbet as a palate freshener between courses.

The traditional course is to fill the orange, grapefruit, lime or lemon with the same flavour sorbet. But why not experiment with a more innovative taste and colour combination, as in the example shown here. Fill the carved orange with delicious raspberry sorbet, then serve with fresh raspberries and garnish with mint leaves.

PREPARING THE CONTAINER

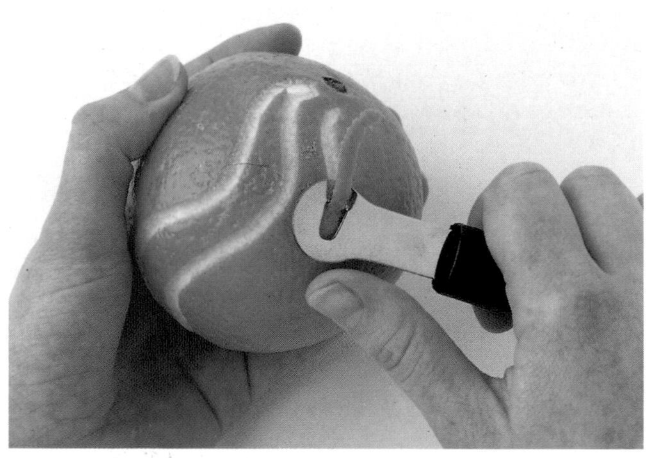

1 Hold a whole orange firmly in one hand. With a grooved cutter, remove thin, wavy strips of peel from top to bottom. If you prefer, you can carve horizontal waves or work in straight lines.

2 Cut off the top of the orange. Use a very sharp, thin-bladed knife to cut round the edge of the flesh to loosen it from the pith and skin. Scoop out the contents with a spoon.

FINISHING TOUCHES

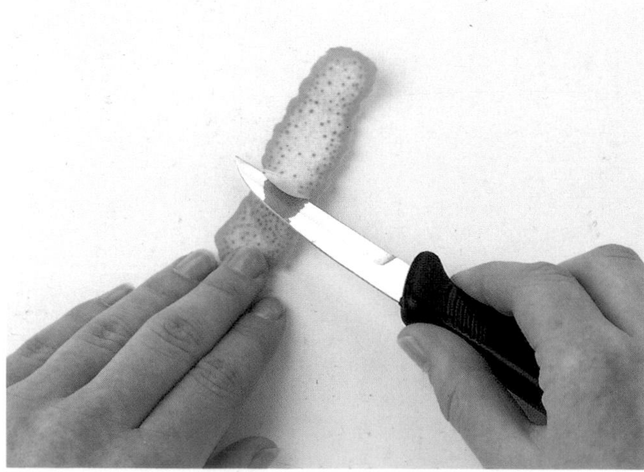

1 Take a strip of orange peel and use a very sharp knife to remove the pith. You can use the grooved-out strips, although they will be rather fiddly to work with and difficult to cut into finer strips.

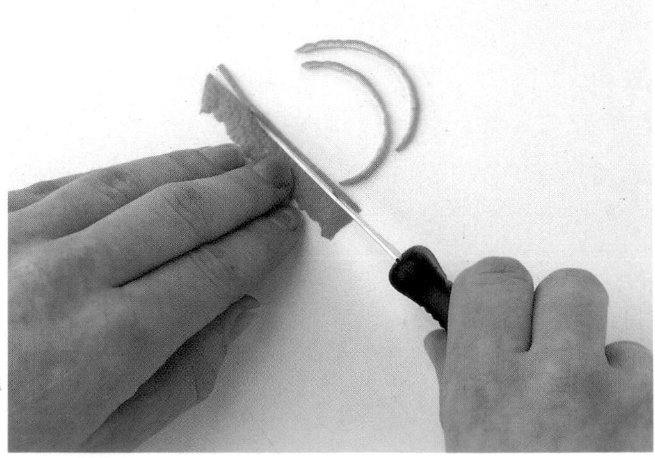

2 With a sharp knife slice the piece of peel into thin strips and use as decoration. If making in advance, boil the strips in sugar and water as the light syrup coating will prevent them shrivelling.

MELON BASKET

Put fruits and vegetables to creative use in a colourful melon and crudité arrangement. It makes a strikingly different centrepiece for a formal dinner or buffet table.

The clean cool colours of fresh fruits and vegetables need little or no extra adornment. In this impressive table centrepiece, which combines fruits and vegetables of all shapes and sizes, they're shown off to maximum mouthwatering effect.

The display is made by simply halving a melon, then preparing raw fruits and vegetables on skewers and pressing these into the melon flesh, contrasting different shapes and colours to form an attractive natural design. Leafy green herbs and courgette flowers are used to fill in any gaps in the display, and enhance its fresh appeal.

Details of the fruits and vegetables used for the display shown above are given overleaf, but you can replace these with your own selection; to keep costs down, use seasonal produce in your arrangement. Select fruits and vegetables that are not too soft and ripe, and choose varied colours for the best results.

▲ *For a table decoration that looks good enough to eat, combine a colourful medley of mouthwatering fruits and vegetables – some shaped into sculptural forms, some left in their natural state.*

MAKING THE MELON BASKET

MATERIALS

Sharp knife

Firm honeydew melon

Dessert spoon

Selection of fruit and vegetables: spring onions, celery, carrots, broccoli, radishes, hard tomatoes, grapes, olives and starfruit

Cocktail sticks

Wooden skewers, long

Fresh leafy green herbs, such as mint

Courgette flowers

1 Use a sharp knife to cut the melon in half, angling the cuts to create a zigzag edge. Scoop out the seeds with a spoon. Slice a little off the base of one half-melon to level it so that it will stand firmly.

2 Slice the stems of the spring onions, celery and carrots lengthways two or three times, finishing the cuts about 2.5cm (1in) before the stalk end. Place in ice cold water so the stems fan out. Break the broccoli into florets, and insert a wooden skewer into each.

3 To prepare the radish flowers, first cut the radishes in half, angling the cuts to create a zigzag edge. Peel a tomato in a spiral, then wrap a length of tomato skin round each half-radish. Secure with a cocktail stick. Insert a wooden skewer into the base of each "flower".

4 Slice the starfruit. Push all the fruits and vegetables on to long wooden skewers. Break the ends off some of the skewers to vary the lengths – if you prefer, you can do this as you assemble the display.

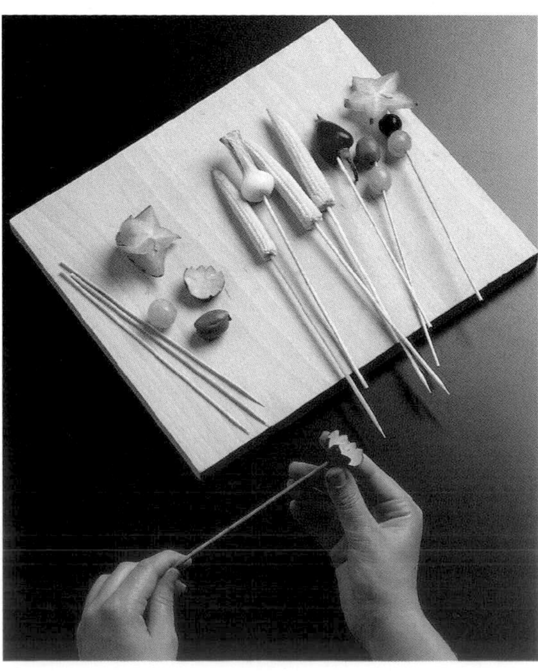

5 Push the sticks into the flesh of the half-melon, and arrange in an attractive way. Fill in the gaps with sprigs of leafy green herbs, such as mint, and bright courgette flowers.

Ice Bowls

Create a stunning table centrepiece for your celebratory dining room with a frosty ice bowl, sparkling with gold stars and glitter, or decorated with colourful, edible flowers.

Impress your guests with this sparkling ice bowl – use it to serve crunchy crudités as a starter, a crisp green salad or a refreshing fruit cocktail.

MAKING THE ICE BOWL

Make sure that the bowls you use are freezer proof, and that you choose a size which will fit easily into your freezer.

MATERIALS

Two glass or plastic bowls of the same shape, one slightly smaller than the other

Filtered tap water or bottled water

Edible flowers

Knitting needle or wooden cocktail stick

Sticky tape

1 PREPARING THE BOWLS
Carefully wash the flowers, picking out any blemished areas. Place the smaller bowl inside the larger one and hold it so there is a gap of about 1.5cm (⅝in) between the two around the sides and bottom. Tape the small bowl in place with pieces of sticky tape around the rim.

2 ADDING THE FIRST LAYER
Fill the gap between the two bowls with water, until the water reaches approximately 2.5cm (1in) up the side of the bowls. Add flowers to the water, one by one, using the knitting needle or cocktail stick to arrange them in an attractive, dense pattern. Push some flowers under the bowl to continue the pattern on the base. Place the bowls in the freezer.

3 ADDING FURTHER LAYERS
When the bottom layer of water has frozen, remove the bowls from the freezer. Add a further 2.5cm (1in) of water and more flowers, using the knitting needle or cocktail stick to arrange them into an attractive pattern, as in step 2. Place the bowls in the freezer. Continue in this way for an even design, building up layers until the bowl is the required depth.

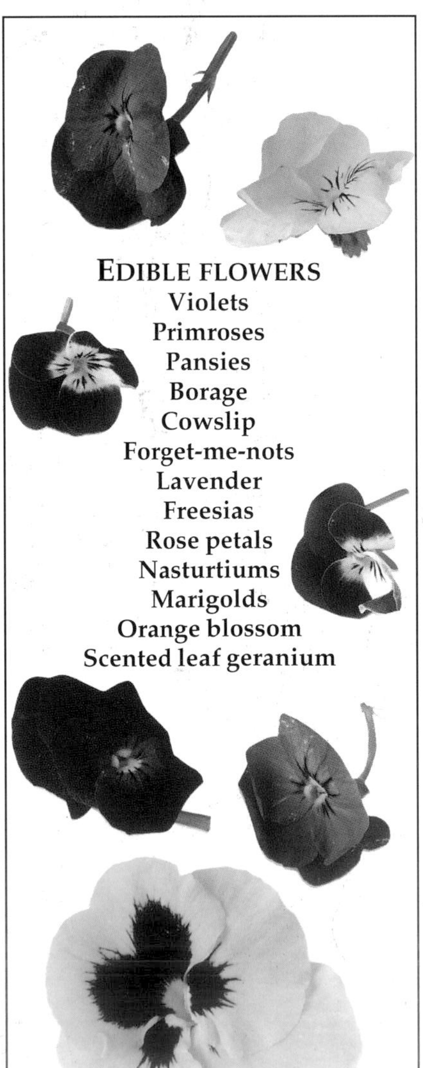

4 REMOVING THE ICE BOWL
When the ice bowl is frozen solid, remove the bowls from the freezer. If you are using plastic bowls, wobble them slightly to separate them from the ice bowl. To remove glass bowls, run tepid water over the inside of the smaller bowl, then gently lift it away; repeat on the large bowl, running tepid water over the outside. Place the ice bowl in the freezer until needed.

DECORATIVE ICE CUBES

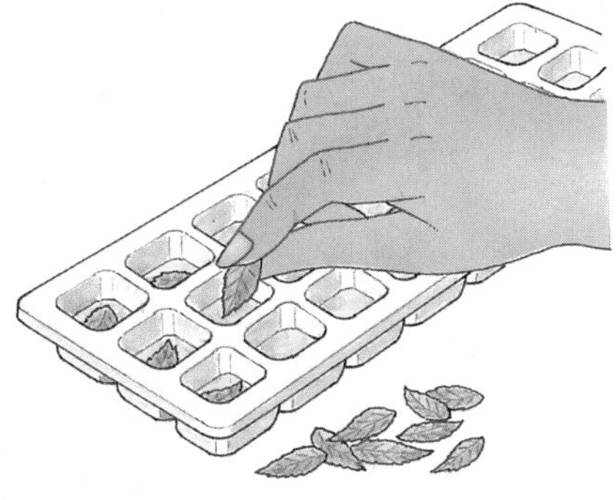

To accompany your ice bowl, create some herb ice-cubes, using fresh sprigs of mint. Select unblemished, fresh mint leaves and carefully wash them. Place a single leaf in the bottom of each section of an ice-cube tray. Half fill the tray with filtered tap or bottled water, so that the leaf floats. Place the tray in the freezer. When the water has frozen, top up each section in the tray and freeze it again.

Floating Candles

Create a fairytale setting for your table by floating flowers and candles in a dish of water. The delicate petals look magical in the flickering candlelight, and the heat of the flames helps to release their delicious scents.

White floating candles, surrounded by pink Ranunculus and Michaelmas daisies create a romantic mood for a special meal.

These beautiful floral water lights take just moments to assemble. Fill a shallow glass container with water and float flowerheads or petals on the surface. Add a couple of tea lights/night-lights or special floating candles. You can buy the candles from department stores, candle suppliers, florists, gift shops and some supermarkets. Tea lights/night-lights are usually white, but floating candles come in several colours, including pink, blue and green.

Make sure the container you choose won't be damaged by the heat of the candles – a pie dish or fruit bowl is ideal. Fairly flat, open flowers look pretty floating on water – try impatiens, nasturtiums, marguerites, geraniums, gerbera, pansies and marigolds.

A single blue floating candle, encircled by fresh daisies, looks striking in a blue ceramic bowl. Group three bowls together for more impact.

A few white Ranunculus flowers and some ivy leaves add life to a single floating candle in a glass sweet dish. Extra greenery in the saucer adds the finishing touch.

Pink roses and tea lights/night-lights float among florets of lacy cow parsley in a shallow glass container. The flowers and candles are a perfect match.

Candlelight Dinner

Celebrate special occasions using the soft, warm glow of candlelight to create a magical atmosphere. Stand candles on the mantelshelf, group them together to create extravagant table centrepieces and decorate them with festive motifs.

Red, green, white and gold are classic colours for Christmas candles. These candles have been decorated with painted or carved seasonal motifs.

Candles really set the scene for special occasions, creating a warm and intimate atmosphere. You can stand them in gleaming brass or pewter candlesticks on the mantelpiece or dinner table, or cluster them together in a bed of evergreen foliage and pine cones to create a sweet-scented display.

Candles will make holiday meals extra special. Place them in elegant candlesticks or candelabras, or use them to create stunning table centrepieces. Try grouping together candles of different sizes on a flat plate or circle of foil, and intersperse them with glittering baubles, tinsel and gold-sprayed fir cones. Alternatively, buy floating candles in red, gold and green, and put them in a glass bowl filled with water – trim the bowl with holly and red winter berries for an extra festive touch.

Remember to take care if you use candles in your home – make sure they're fixed in a firm support, out of the reach of young children, and that you extinguish them before you go out or to bed. As an extra precaution, it's worth installing a smoke alarm.

Festive foliage *A touch of winter foliage adds a festive air to these two sturdy, white candles. The red berries and holly and ivy leaves are simply tied around the base of each candle with strands of natural raffia. Two handsome wrought iron candle-holders support the candles and stop the wax from dripping on to the mantelpiece.*

You could copy this idea using dainty sprigs of dried flowers instead of foliage, for a softer, prettier look.

Put on the glitz
Dress up a candelabra to transform it into a striking display piece for your mantelshelf or dinner table. This classic, verdigris candelabra has been hung with large and small Christmas baubles, in exotic sapphire blue and copper. The baubles are simply tied on to the arms and stem of the candelabra with silky satin ribbon.

Sparkling Christmas decorations, like baubles and tinsel, are always shown off to the full in candlelight, as they reflect the dancing flames.

Studded in style *Tiny gold studs cover the sides of these white candles, making them look much more festive. The studs are just pressed into the wax at random or in simple patterns. You can buy studs or clamps like these, shaped into circles, squares, stars and hearts, from jewellery findings stockists. Use a pin to lightly imprint the position of the studs on the candle before you press them in.*

Self-contained
Coloured glass tumblers and highball glasses make clever containers for short, wide candles and tea lights/night-lights. Just sit the candles inside, where they'll give off a magical, coloured glow. Here, blue and yellow glasses of different heights have been grouped together to create an interesting table centrepiece. They're placed on a piece of silver foil, which reflects the sparkle of the flames.

Decorator's delight

Candles are great fun to decorate – especially for Christmas. You can stencil them with festive motifs, such as fir trees, stars and snowflakes, paint them freehand with colourful stripes and dots, or lightly sponge them with gold or silver paint. Alternatively, carve patterns into the wax to create subtle, textured designs.

You can also use pretty trimmings to smarten up candles and their holders for the festivities. Stick dried flowers around the base of a candle, or bind it with a fancy ribbon; remember to blow out the candle or remove the trimmings before the candle burns down to them. Trim candle-holders with sparkling tinsel, baubles and streams of spiralling gift wrap ribbon, or with miniature dried flower swags.

***Candlelit menu** A menu carefully written out on handmade paper, available from craft stores, backed with cardboard and decorated with ribbons and herbs adds a delightful touch to your candlelit dinner.*

***Gilded centrepiece** This splendid display is simply formed from sparkling Christmas decorations, grouped around plain white candles, placed on a gold-sprayed doily.*

***Evergreen wreath** A traditional Christmas wreath is easy to make from blue spruce, holly, ivy and pine cones. Stand some slender candles in amongst the foliage, but make sure they aren't allowed to burn right down to the bottom.*

DRESSING CANDELABRAS

Create a decorative centrepiece for a special occasion by dressing simple candelabras with flowers, ribbons and jewels.

Candlesticks and candelabras are one of the most decorative of all home accessories, and make ideal table centrepieces for celebration suppers. Although their functional role has long been eclipsed by technology, they are as popular as ever. The flickering light of many candles will transform even the most pedestrian surroundings – areas of soft light and pools of velvety dark shadow conjure up the romance of a more leisurely age.

You can customize plain candlesticks and candelabras for special occasions: match them to your table setting, the room scheme or a birthday or wedding cake. Use translucent and shiny materials that reflect and scatter the light – try glass beads, metallic ribbons and chains, foils and paints.

Slim fabric ribbon in lush velvet or printed satin works effectively if you want to coordinate a range of different candlesticks for a large celebration. Simple bows, tied around the base of a candlestick or the branches of a candelabra, make ideal decorative details for a wedding supper.

Candlelight is wonderfully forgiving, so the simplest embellishments will turn your table into a fairytale banquet.

▲ ***Glorious greenery*** *Delicate foliage and floral stems, picked fresh from the garden or selected from a large bouquet, add real elegance to a forged metal candelabra. Secure them to the branches with florists' wire.*

Gossamer swathes *Silver fuse wire, threaded with tiny glass beads then looped and twisted into web-like strands, transforms a a wrought iron candelabra into a gothic centrepiece. Copper wire, florists' wire and bonsai wire make equally effective candle webs, and can be strung with all manner of pretty jewel-like items.*

All that glisters *Lend a plain candelabra a look of opulence with old costume jewellery, wired to the cups and branches with florists' wire. Multi-faceted glass beads, in the form of necklaces, earrings and bracelets, catch the light in the manner of a chandelier, and scatter pretty colours across the room.*

Bedecked and beribboned *Pretty patterned ribbon adds festive elegance to a formal candelabra. Short bands, secured with double-sided tape, embellish the candle cups, while each of the branches has its own soft bow. When using fabrics close to candle flames, it's a good idea to spray them with a proprietary flameproofer, available from sewing departments.*

FLORAL CANDELABRAS

Rich spirals of colourful flowers and dark, glossy leaves transform a pair of plain candlesticks into a sumptuous and stylish dinner table decoration. Use an assortment of flowers in season to set the mood for spring, summer, winter or autumn parties.

Even beginners can make these pretty candlestick garlands. They appear to twist around the candlestick but in fact they simply curve up the front.

CANDLESTICK GARLANDS

Extravagant in style, yet simple to make, this combination of flowers and candlelight creates the perfect dinner party atmosphere.

Use plain candlesticks, as ornate or highly decorative ones will merely detract from the flowers. Plain china, brass, pewter or even plastic candlesticks are all suitable for this effect, and if you don't have any, they're not too expensive to buy.

Select seasonal flowers to save on expense. Better still, choose some from the garden. Roses, viburnum, mimosa, Ranunculus, anemones, golden rod and laurel will make well-proportioned garlands, but don't be frightened to experiment with any mix. You'll need a lot of flowers – a luscious garland for even the smallest candlestick requires quite a number of blooms.

It's best to make up the garlands on the day of the dinner, but you can make them the previous day – just remember to mist them well with water and then store them in wet tissue paper in an airtight container.

MATERIALS

Assortment of fresh flowers and foliage

Candlesticks

20 gauge florists' wire

Silver reel wire

Green florists' tape (gutta percha)

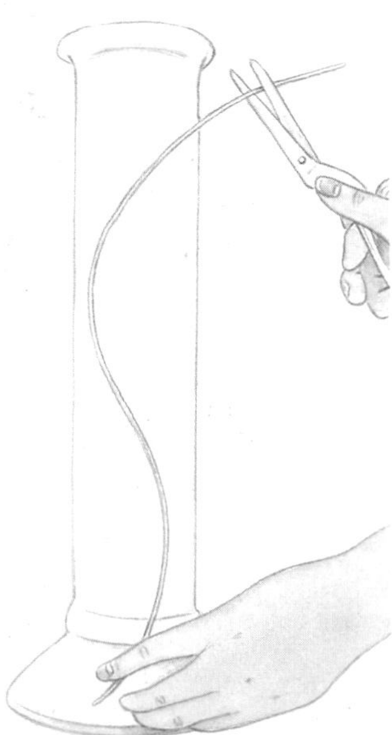

1 MAKING THE BASE
Measure a length of florists' wire against the candlestick, allowing for it to twist slightly up the candleholder.

2 BINDING THE WIRE
Cut the florists' wire to this length. Bind it with green florists' tape, wrapping the tape over and over until it covers the wire completely.

3 STARTING THE GARLAND
Begin by placing a large piece of foliage at the top of the covered wire. Tie it in place with a short piece of silver reel wire.

4 MAKING THE POSIES
Gather up a small posy of flowers and foliage and bind the stems together with silver reel wire. Add the posy to the covered wire, binding it in place with silver reel wire.

5 FORMING THE GARLAND
Continue to wrap little posies of flowers and foliage along the length of the covered wire, checking that there are no gaps. Hold the garland against the candleholder and, as you approach the base, attach the posies so that they point in opposite directions. To cover the end of the wire, use a large piece of foliage, to match the foliage at the top.

6 FINISHING OFF
When you have completed the garland, position it so that it curves gently up the side of the candlestick. Then, starting at the top of the candlestick, secure the garland with three or four short lengths of silver reel wire, twisting the ends of the wire together and tucking them under the foliage, out of sight.

Decoupage Candleholders

Turn glass containers into glorious garden candleholders with a patchwork of fine coloured paper. When the candles are alight, they scatter a beautiful, jewel-like glow over their surroundings.

You can use any smooth glass container to make the pretty candleholders featured here. Glass jars, pots, bowls and vases in all shapes and sizes are ideal, provided the neck is wide enough to take a votive candle or tea light/night-light, and that there is no risk of the container toppling over.

To decorate the container, you simply stick paper shapes on to the outside of the glass, then seal the design in place with a coat of varnish. Coloured tissue paper or handmade translucent paper are the most effective choice, but they are fragile when wet and care must be taken not to tear them when applying the adhesive. You can strengthen thin papers by applying a protective sealer before use. To prevent the paper from fading, avoid exposing your finished container to direct sunlight. Coloured tissue paper and handmade papers are available from stationers, craft shops and art suppliers.

For a different look, you could use special Victorian-style paper decals or motifs cut from giftwrap for the decoupage. Or apply just a few motifs here and there and leave some areas bare – this is particularly effective on coloured glass containers. On a safety note, never leave a lighted candle unattended.

▲ *Add a warm, welcoming glow to an outdoor summer party with a group of glass candleholders decorated with jewel-coloured tissue paper. Here, a large candleholder makes a dramatic table centrepiece, while small holders provide soft background lighting.*

MATERIALS

Glass container
Tissue paper or translucent handmade paper
Acrylic spray sealer
Scissors, or craft knife and cutting mat
PVA adhesive
Small paintbrush or sponge applicator
Acrylic clear spray varnish
Votive candle or tea light/night-light

BEFORE YOU START

Make sure your glass container is clean and dry both inside and out. Coat the back of your chosen papers with acrylic spray sealer before cutting out the shapes, to strengthen them and to prevent them becoming transparent when you apply the glue. You should spray thin paper on both sides, allowing one side to dry before turning it over.

1 Cut the tissue paper or handmade paper into small pieces, varying the shapes and sizes to suit your container. Apply a thin coat of PVA adhesive to one side of one piece, using a small paintbrush or sponge applicator. The adhesive is white when applied, but dries clear.

2 Position the first piece of paper on the outside of the container and gently smooth it in place with your finger. Continue like this, overlapping pieces as desired until you have covered the entire container. Wrap the top pieces over the upper edge of the container.

3 If you wish, cut out a few extra motifs from paper to add a more decorative finish; here, squares are used to form a band of diamonds round the centre of the container. Apply the motifs with PVA adhesive, positioning them as desired over the previously decoupaged area. Leave to dry thoroughly.

4 Apply a light coat of clear spray varnish in gloss, satin or matt, depending on the finish desired; leave to dry, then apply a second coat of varnish for a more hard-wearing finish. Place a votive candle or tea light/night-light in the centre of the container, anchoring it securely to the base, if necessary, to prevent it from toppling over.

Festive Flair

Celebrate the festive season in style this year by creating a Christmas tree as a centrepiece. Make decorations in paper or fabric, hang the tree with fruits, sweets and flowers, or use bold and unusual colours – anything goes at Christmas time.

This small fir tree makes a festive table-top display. It's hung with homemade paper decorations and candles that cast a warm glow over the feast.

FESTIVE TARTANS

Tartan is the perfect choice for making and trimming traditional decorations at Christmas and other winter festivities. There's a whole wealth of clever ideas for jazzing up your table: tie large tartan bows to dress up your table-top, or to add to seasonal wreaths, swags and table centre arrangements; or make your own Christmas tree trims from scraps of tartan fabric. Make your Christmas and New Year celebrations a truly Scottish affair with a combination of colourful makes and place setting ideas.

Ribbon-wrapped

A basket planted with hyacinths takes on a festive air and makes a charming table decoration when you bind the handle with ribbon. Wind a single length of ribbon around the handle from one end to the other, binding in the ends to secure; then take two separate lengths of ribbon and tie one in a bow at each end of the handle. Choose a tartan ribbon that tones with the hyacinths – here, purple and gold checks are a perfect foil for mauve hyacinths.

Mini tote bags *Use up scraps of tartan fabric to make little favours to hang on your Christmas tree centrepiece or to set at each place for a holiday meal. Trim the bags with a tassel and matching cord and fill them with a small gift, chocolates or piney potpourri.*

Table dressing *A tartan place mat and pretty ribbon trims set off tartan crockery in great style. Add a deliciously aromatic touch by making your own favours from a square of fabric with a net window and filling them with spicy, seasonal potpourri.*

Painted Plates

Try out your painting skills on plain china, and produce a set of stunning painted plates. There are four designs for you to copy – sunflowers, harlequin diamonds, hearts and polka dots – and they're all as easy as painting by numbers.

Your hand-painted plates will look wonderful displayed on a dresser like this one, grouped on a shelf or hung on special plate hooks on your wall.

HEARTS PLATE

For this hearts design, you'll need to buy some adhesive masking film from an artists' supplier or a craft shop.

MATERIALS

Unglazed white china plate

Water-based ceramic paints in blue and red

Matt or gloss acrylic varnish, or PVA woodworking glue

Broad, flat artists' brush

Fine, round artists' brush

Old bowl for mixing paint

Adhesive masking film

Packet of self-adhesive spots

Tracing paper and carbon paper

Compass, ruler and pencil

Scissors and craft knife

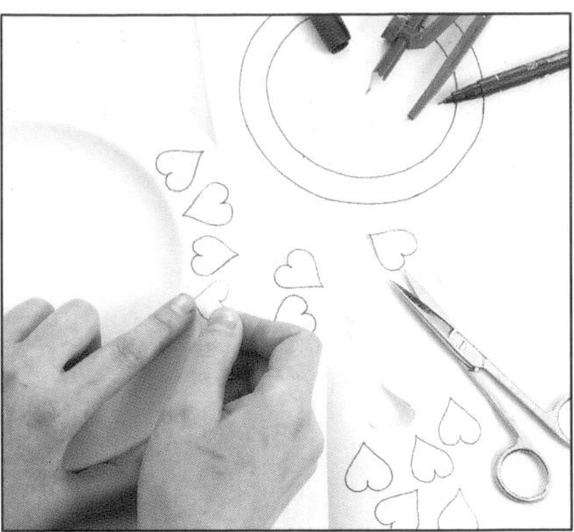

1 PREPARING THE TEMPLATES
Measure the diameter of the plate just inside the rim. Using the compass and pencil, draw a circle a little smaller than this on to the adhesive masking film. Draw another circle, 12mm (½in) smaller, inside it. Cut out the ring and stick it centrally on the plate. Draw a small heart and trace it about 30 times. Using carbon paper, transfer the hearts on to the masking film. Cut them out then stick them round the rim of the plate and in the centre.

2 PAINTING THE BACKGROUND
Using the broad, flat artists' brush, paint the entire plate blue. Leave the paint to dry thoroughly, then peel off the masking film.

3 PAINTING THE HEARTS
Stick self-adhesive spots around the unpainted ring, spacing them evenly. Then stick another one in the centre of the plate. Using the fine, round artists' brush, paint the hearts red. In an old bowl, mix red and blue paint to create purple, and use this to paint the ring. Leave the paint to dry.

4 COMPLETING THE PLATE
Using the craft knife, lift up the edges of the spots and peel them off. Using the fine round artists' brush, paint the spots red. Leave the paint to dry, then apply a couple of coats of varnish or diluted PVA, as in POLKA DOTS PLATE, step 4.

To recreate this pretty flower plate, copy the flower a few times on to adhesive masking film. Cut out the flowers and stick them on the plate. Paint the plate, then peel off the flowers and paint them. Seal the design with varnish.

Sgraffito Wooden Chargers

Sgraffito is a form of incised decoration which can be used to embellish almost any surface. Apply it to a set of wooden chargers to add individuality and style to place settings.

The term 'sgraffito' is derived from the Italian *sgraffire* – to scratch – and describes a traditional decorative technique which is commonly used for house decoration, ceramics and in fine art. A tinted layer of paint or glaze is applied over a white basecoat (or vice versa) and a design is then scratched into the top layer revealing the lower layer. Sgraffito can be used to apply almost any linear design, from bold repeating geometrics and free-flowing arabesques to leaves, flowers and even animal forms.

In the project on the following pages, sgraffito decoration is applied to wooden chargers – large plates designed to sit under dinner plates as a form of decoration and to protect the table surface. The design is based on a simple freehand leaf form, but you can adapt the technique to a design of your choice. Sgraffito decoration can be applied over the entire surface, but for this project the motif is masked off using sticky-back plastic which is readily available from craft suppliers and do-it-yourself stores.

For the best results, use car paints to apply the decoration to the chargers. These are tough and hold the traced sgrafitto line particularly well, but you should avoid bringing food into direct contact with the painted plates. The chargers are finished with two coats of hardwearing car lacquer. Car lacquer and car paint is available in pens, touch-up pots and sprays from car accessory shops and some do-it-yourself stores. After use, wipe the chargers down with a damp cloth rather than submerging them in water.

▲ *Stylized leaf motifs with a tracery of incised sgraffito decoration add a flourish to plain wooden underplates. The dark blue-green pattern looks crisp and clear against the matt white ground, and gives the chargers a bright, contemporary feel.*

SGRAFFITO DECORATION ON WOODEN CHARGERS

MATERIALS

Wooden charger

Wet-and-dry sandpaper, fine grade

Protective face mask

Car spray paint, white

Sticky-back plastic contact paper

Felt-tipped pen

Craft knife

Touch-up pot(s) of car paint, in the colour(s) of your choice

Pointed tool, such as darts arrow

Spray car laquer

BEFORE YOU START

The sgraffito technique demands minimal drawing skills, but it is still a good idea to practise drawing the motifs on paper before you start. Choose abstract shapes such as squares, triangles and circles, or go for organic forms such as leaves and flowers. Find suitable motifs on ceramics, wallpaper and fabrics. The sgraffito decoration is also easy to work, but you will find it useful to experiment with different ways of filling the motifs. Practise in pencil on scrap paper. You can use abstract patterns like hatching and cross-hatching, or base it on natural forms such as the veining of leaves.

1 Prepare the surface of the charger by sanding it with fine-grade wet-and-dry paper. This roughens the surface and provides a key for the paint.

2 Take the charger out of doors, prop it up so that it is almost vertical and use a spray can of car paint to prime the surface. Cover adjacent areas to protect them from the paint mist, and wear a mask. Leave to dry, and apply another coat of paint to create a solid paint layer. Leave to dry thoroughly.

▲ *Bright lacquer red and cool sea-green make an eyecatching combination. The stylized foliate motif has been incised with regular, freehand hatching to create a barely perceptible texture which contrasts with the smooth finish of the spray-painted background.*

3 Cut out two rectangles of sticky-back plastic and remove the protective backing. Apply it to the surface of the plate, sticky side down, over the areas on which you intend to place the motifs. Press the plastic down so that it adheres firmly to the paint surface.

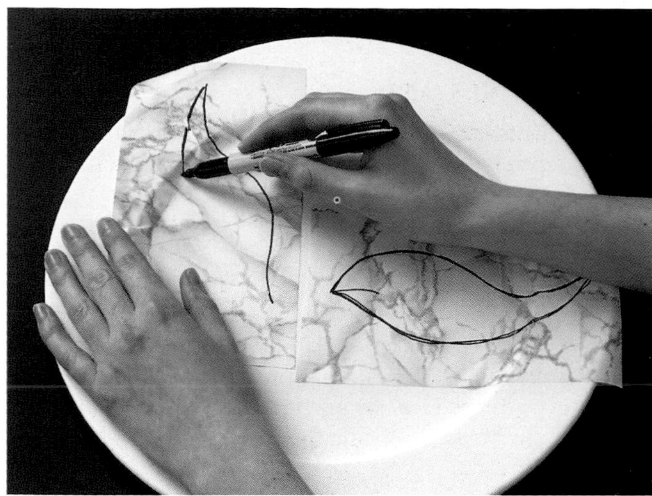

4 Use a felt-tipped pen to draw a leaf motif – or other motif of your choice – freehand on to each piece of the sticky-back plastic. Keep to simple shapes that are easy to draw.

5 Use a sharp craft knife to cut out the leaf shapes – the plastic cuts easily if the blade is sharp. Remove the cut-out sticky-back plastic motifs – the remaining plastic will act as a mask while you apply the paint.

6 Paint the cut-out leaf shape within the sticky-back plastic using a touch-up pot of car paint; use the brush applicator in the top of the pot to apply the paint. Paint one motif only, because it is important that the paint film doesn't dry before you proceed to the next stage.

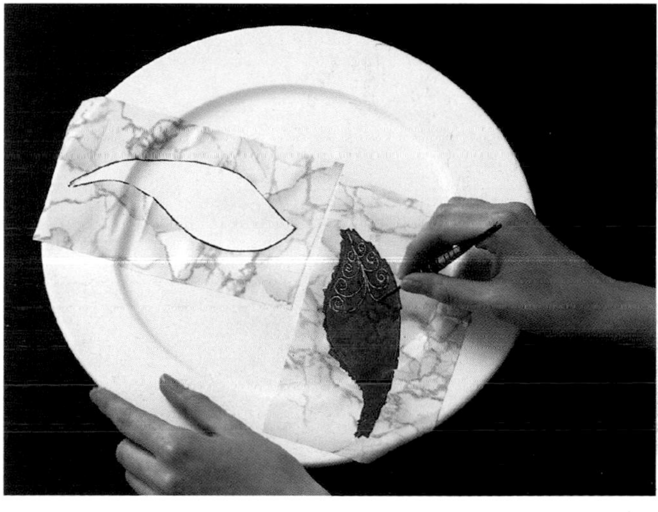

7 While the paint is still wet, use a pointed tool such as a darts arrow to draw a sgrafitto design, freehand, into the surface. Here, scrolling leaf 'veins' are marked. Work quickly before the paint dries.

8 Allow the paint to dry thoroughly (10-15 minutes). Remove the plastic mask and check the effect. If you are pleased with it, repeat steps 6-8 for the other motif.

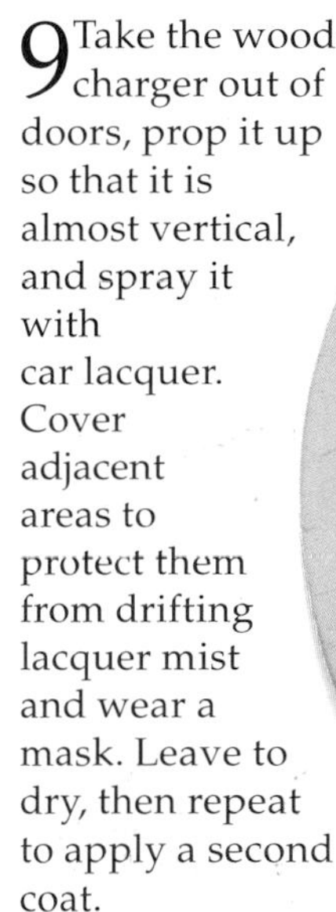

9 Take the wooden charger out of doors, prop it up so that it is almost vertical, and spray it with car lacquer. Cover adjacent areas to protect them from drifting lacquer mist and wear a mask. Leave to dry, then repeat to apply a second coat.

A dresser is the ideal place to store and display a set of decorated underplates when they are not in use, but a long shelf at picture rail height will also allow you to show them as a set. Give the plates a one-off hand-crafted feel by varying the way you interpret the basic motif from plate to plate.

Sgraffito wooden chargers will enhance any table setting and provide a heat-resistant, non-slip base for dinner plates. Choose colours and themes to coordinate with your room scheme. Remember you should never use the chargers as dinner plates – they are purely decorative and shouldn't come into direct contact with food.

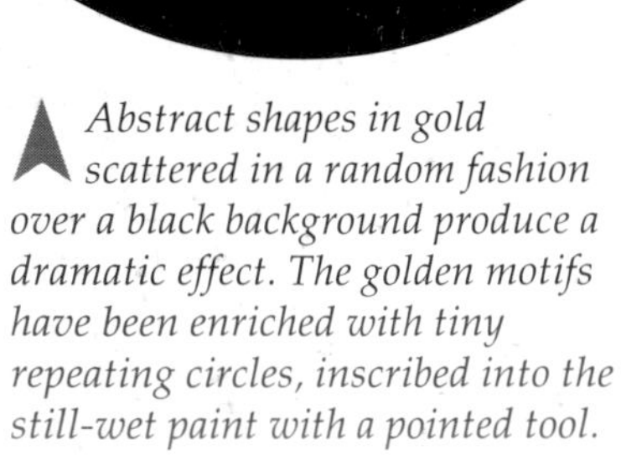

Abstract shapes in gold scattered in a random fashion over a black background produce a dramatic effect. The golden motifs have been enriched with tiny repeating circles, inscribed into the still-wet paint with a pointed tool.

Gilded Glassware

Add shimmering gold detailing to glass plates for a truly festive look. Use the plates as decorative underplates to enhance your dinner service.

Beaded edging

You can give cheap glass plates a gold bobbled edge by simply sticking on gold or bronze beads at 1.5cm (⅝in) intervals, using instant bonding adhesive.

The bobble-edged plates featured here have had tiny gold stars scattered round the rims, and their bobbled edges coloured with gold felt-tipped pen. All this detailing is easily removable – just wipe off the felt-tipped pen with lighter fuel and brush off the stars.

You can buy plain and coloured bobble-edged plates from some glassware and kitchenware stockists and department stores.

Gilded detailing gives these glass plates an extra sparkle. None of the detailing is permanent – the gold ink can be wiped off with lighter fuel and the stars simply brush off.

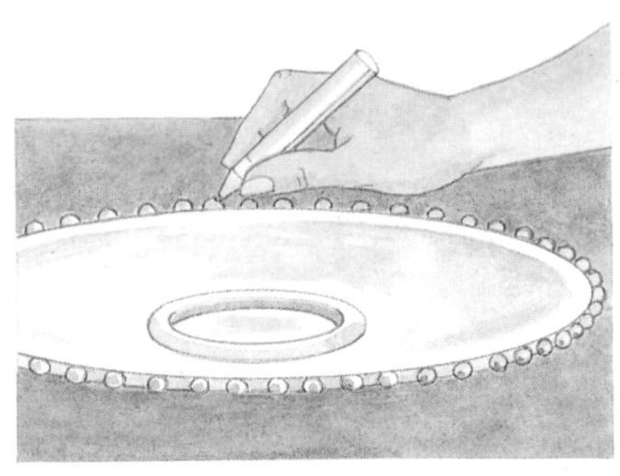

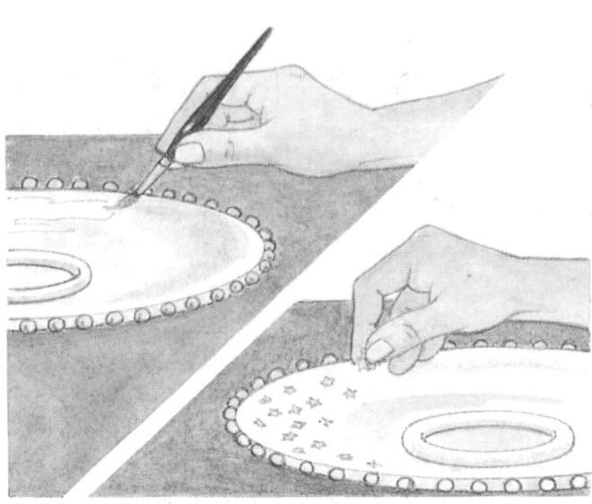

MATERIALS

Bobble-edged glass plates
Gold felt-tipped pen
Tiny gold foil stars
Fine watercolour brush
Jar of water
Clean cloth
Newspaper to cover work surface
Lighter fuel

1 GILDING THE BOBBLES
Using the felt-tip pen, colour in the gold bobbles around the edges of the plates, colouring in all the bobbles on some plates, and alternate bobbles on others (make sure there is an even number of bobbles if you're colouring in alternate ones). Use a cloth moistened with lighter fuel to clean up any smudges. Leave the ink to dry thoroughly before use.

2 ADDING THE STARS
Using the watercolour brush, apply a little water round the outer rim of a plate. Sprinkle the tiny stars over the dampened area. Press them down lightly with the brush. On another plate, apply water in a swirl across the plate and sprinkle on a 'Milky Way' of stars. Repeat to decorate all the plates with stars in this way.

➤ *Add a flourish with party favours in flamboyant wrappings, using tissue paper, net, foil stars and giftwrap ribbon. Place the favour in a square box, and wrap it in bright tissue paper. Cut two large squares of net in different toning shades, like these dark and pale greens, and lay one over the other. Centre the box over the net and pull up the edges all round, securing them with a rubber band. Cover the band with gold and yellow giftwrap ribbons, curling the ends with a scissor blade. Slip different sizes of gold stars into the net.*

Bonbonnières

A few sugar-coated almonds, wrapped in a wisp of tulle, create an enchanting table gift for christenings, weddings and special anniversary celebrations.

A marriage made in heaven *Pretty bonbonnières, cut from a petal-shaped template, are trimmed with sprigs of pastel flowers to match the wedding colour scheme.*

Bonbonnières are traditional gifts, once given by European aristocrats to celebrate rites of passage such as births, weddings, christenings and special anniversaries. These precious bundles once contained pieces of gold, pearls and jewels, but today almonds coated in sugar are the usual contents. Five only are used, each almond representing health, wealth, happiness, long life or fertility. You can buy sugar-coated almonds – or dragées – in pastel shades, silver and gold. Some specialist confectioners stock them in more vibrant colours, too, such as Christmas reds and greens.

Fine tulle is the best material to use for wrapping the sweets, as net is too stiff. To make the bonbonnières, cut a circular template, roughly 22cm (9in) in diameter, attach several layers of tulle with a pin, and cut out. Sit the almonds in clear plastic or china dishes and wrap a layer of tulle around them. Secure with a length of narrow ribbon.

Starstruck
Silver star and glitter-threaded tulle make extra-special dressings for celebration gifts. Tiny ribbon roses, wired to the trailing silken bows, reflect the colour of the silvered almonds within.

Organza extravaganza
Spotted tulle or organza with crinkle-cut edges makes a delicate sweet wrapping with a difference. Fine rainbow ribbon, used to gather the organza, tones with the pretty pastel shades of the sugared almonds.

Golden shower *Gold leaf almonds nestle in star-scattered tulle, like glittering nuggets of fairy treasure, all tied up with matching bows. These exquisite confectionery favours make perfect table gifts, and are ideal for christenings, coming of age, or golden wedding celebrations.*

Party Favours

For an extra special treat, set a small present by each place setting, wrapped in brightly coloured paper and decorated with pretty handmade paper flowers. The freesias shown here are easy to make from pink and yellow tissue paper.

Four stems of pink and yellow paper freesias, tied with ribbon, add a delicate touch to this gift, wrapped in a sunny yellow handmade paper.

PAPER ROSES

The roses shown here were made from pink Japanese paper, but you can use any soft paper, such as crêpe or tissue. You can buy the wire for the stems from craft shops and florists.

MATERIALS

Soft pink paper
Lightweight green paper
Fine wire
Cotton wool
Gutta-percha tape
Green covered wire
All-purpose household glue
Tracing paper and pencil
Card for the templates
Scissors and secateurs

1 GETTING STARTED
Cut a 25cm (10in) length of fine wire and bend the end into a hook. Glue a small ball of cotton wool, approximately 1cm (⅜in) in diameter, over the hook. Trace the rose centre, petal, leaf and sepal templates on to card and cut them out.

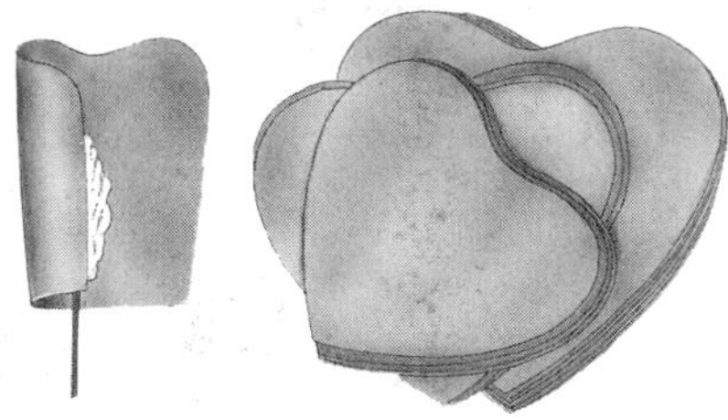

2 MAKING THE ROSE CENTRE
Using the templates, cut one rose centre, four small, three medium and six large petals from the pink paper. Dab glue along the lower edge of the rose centre and wrap it around the cotton wool to form a tube, squeezing the lower edges together.

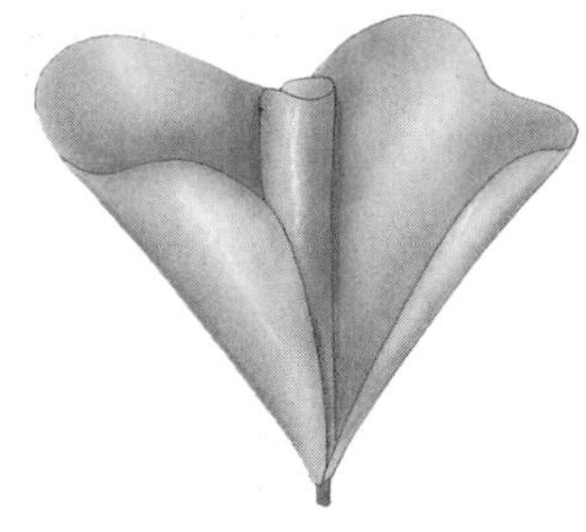

3 ADDING THE SMALL PETALS
Gently pull the rounded ends of the petals over a scissor blade to curl them outwards. Dab glue on to the pointed end of two small petals, and stick one on each side of the flower centre. Glue the remaining two small petals between the first two petals in the same way.

4 COMPLETING THE ROSE
Dab glue on to the pointed end of the three medium petals, and glue them around the small petals, overlapping the petal edges. Glue the six large petals around the medium ones in the same way.

5 ADDING THE SEPALS
From the green paper, cut one set of sepals. Pull the tips of the sepals over a scissor blade to curl them outwards. Dab glue on to the centre and lower edge of the sepals and glue them in place under the rose, wrapping the sepals around the wire to form a conical shape.

6 MAKING THE LEAVES
From the green paper, cut five leaves. Fold each leaf in half along the dotted line, then open them out again. Cut five 10cm (4in) lengths of green covered wire. Glue a length of wire to the centre underside of each leaf, along the fold line. Bunch the leaves together as shown, with two leaves splaying out at each side of a central leaf.

7 ADDING THE LEAVES
Dab glue on to one end of the gutta-percha tape and press this end against the base of the sepals. Bind the tape around the flower stem, adding the leaves about 7.5cm (3in) below the flower head. Bend the leaves outwards. Repeat steps 1-6 to make more flowers.

ROSE TEMPLATES

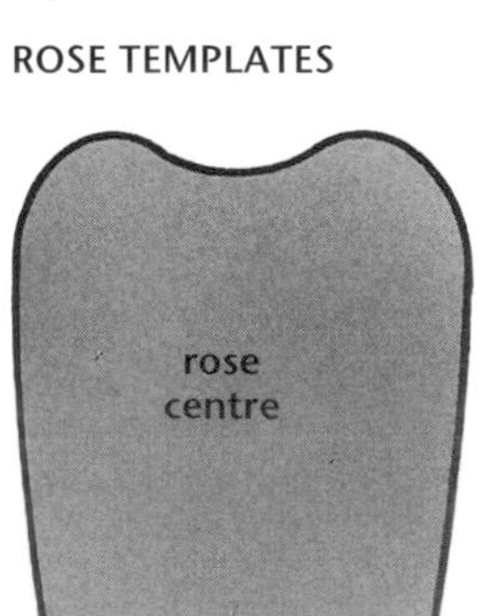

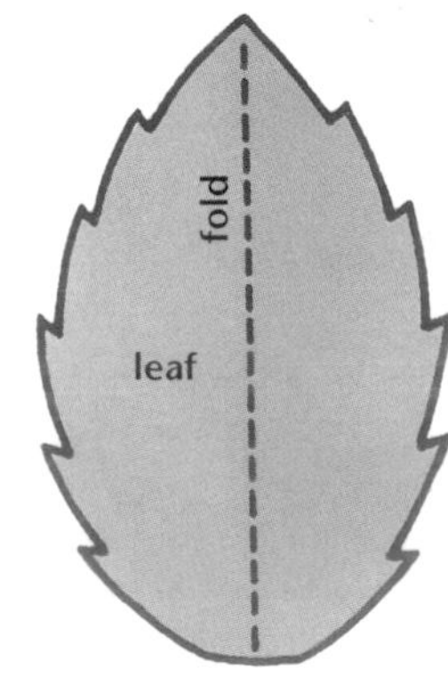

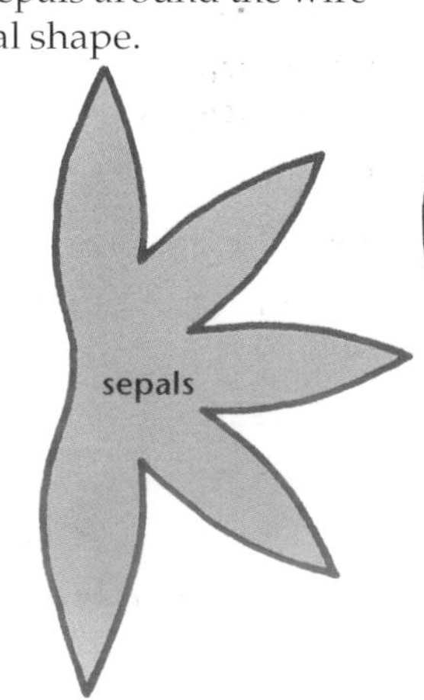

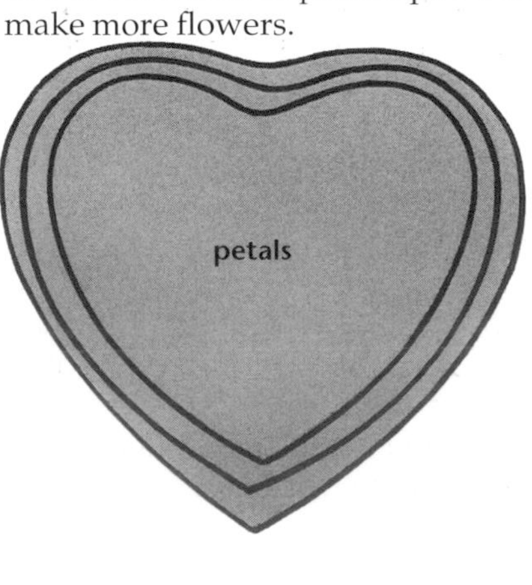

PAPER ANEMONES

These colourful anemones look fantastic in a bright vase or jug. You can make the flowers to match the container for a coordinated look.

Fresh anemones are big and bright, so make your paper anemones in vibrant colours to imitate the real ones.

The petals and leaves are made from crêpe paper which you can buy in most stationery shops: it's best to use double crêpe paper rather than single crêpe paper because it's less likely to tear when you are curling and moulding it into shape.

You'll need a few specialist materials to make the flowers – they're sold by florists. For the anemone stems you'll need special wire flower stems which

you can buy on a reel. You'll also need fine gauge florists' wire to attach the leaves and petals, although you could use the wire flower stems instead. For the flower centres, use cotton balls painted black, or balls of black crêpe paper.

When you've assembled the flowers, you'll need to wrap the stems with a special green sticky tape called gutta tape. This gives the stems a realistic colour and helps to anchor the petals and leaves.

MATERIALS

Crêpe paper in yellow, violet, pale green, deep rose, black and white

Gutta tape

Cotton balls

Black paint or black felt-tipped pen

28cm (11in) wire flower stems

Fine gauge florists' wire

Scissors and small pliers

Clear contact adhesive

Pastel crayons (optional)

1 MAKING THE CENTRE With the pliers, bend over the end of a wire stem and push it into a cotton ball. Secure it with adhesive. Paint the cotton ball black, or colour it with a felt-tipped pen.

TEMPLATES

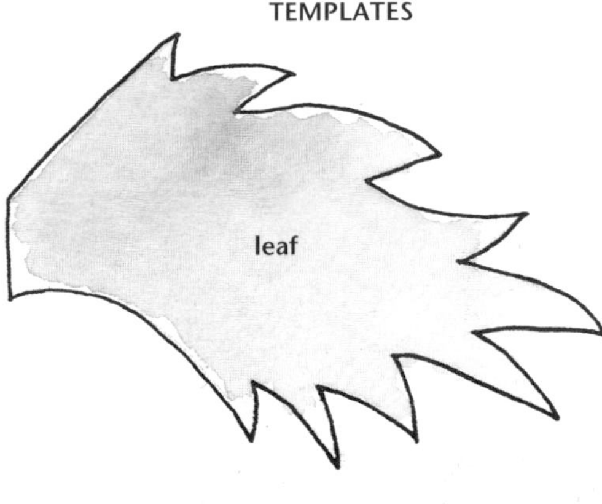

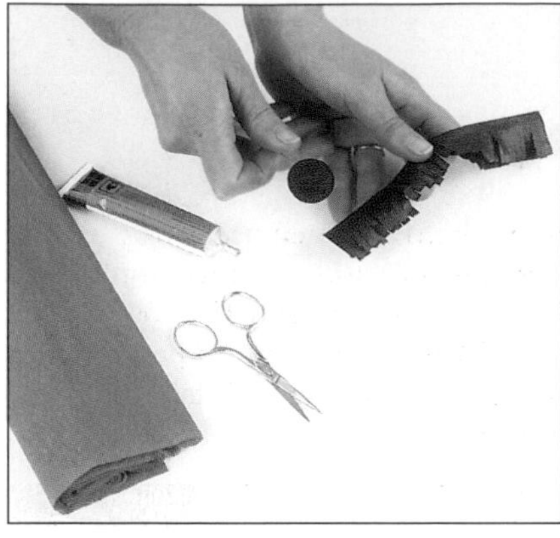

2 APPLYING THE STAMENS Using the stamen template, cut one shape from the black crêpe paper. Cut the fringe and dab adhesive along the opposite edge. Position it around the cotton ball and stem.

3 MAKING THE PETALS Using the petal template, cut out six petals in the colour of your choice. Then, using your thumbs, gently stretch each petal in the centre to create a realistic curved shape.

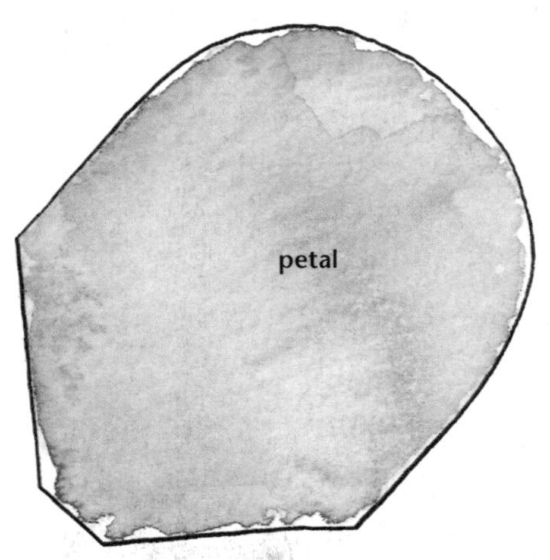

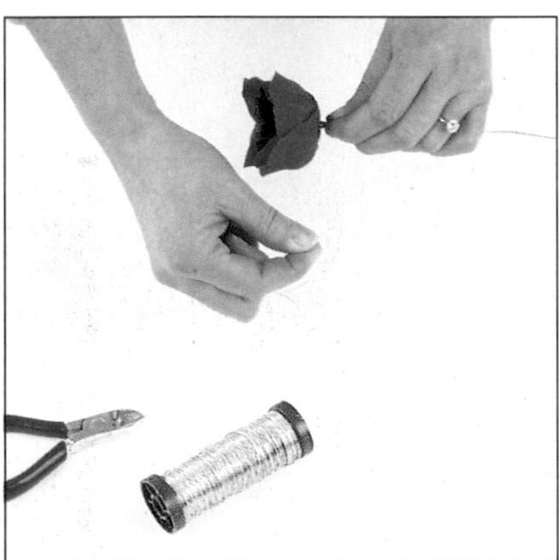

4 ARRANGING THE PETALS Position the six petals around the cotton ball and stamens, arranging them in two rows of three, with the petals slightly overlapping.

5 ATTACHING THE PETALS Dab a little adhesive on to the base of each petal. Then, using the fine florists' wire, firmly bind the petals to the stem.

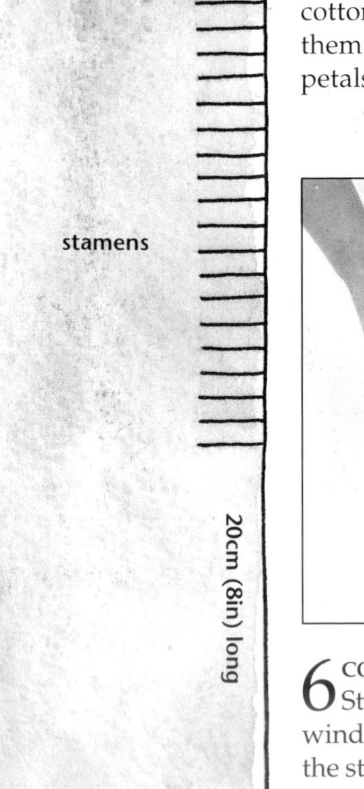

6 COVERING THE STEM Starting at the base of the petals, wind the gutta tape around and down the stem. Keeping the tape taut, continue until all the wire is covered, easing out any creases as you go.

7 ADDING THE LEAVES Using the leaf template, cut three leaves from the green crêpe paper. Wire them to the stem and cover the joins with gutta tape. If you like, use a pastel crayon to add fine leaf veins.

PAPER CARNATIONS AND ASTERS

These colourful paper carnations and asters make a sensational table centrepiece for a special occasion and, as with all paper flowers, have the added advantage of being everlasting. After the dinner party, use them to brighten up a dark corner where house plants won't flourish. They are easy to make from folded strips of tissue and paper napkins, plus a few florists' materials.

PAPER CARNATIONS

Make these super carnations from paper tissues or napkins in realistic soft shades, like peach, pink, white and rosy red. You'll also need some split bamboo canes or green garden sticks, florists' tape and binding wire, which are available from florists.

MATERIALS

Two-ply paper tissues and/or napkins in peach, white, red and shades of pink

Deep pink waterproof artists' ink

30cm (12in) long split bamboo canes or green garden sticks

Binding wire

12mm (½in) wide pale green florists' tape

Pinking shears and scissors

Artists' paintbrush

Ruler or measuring tape

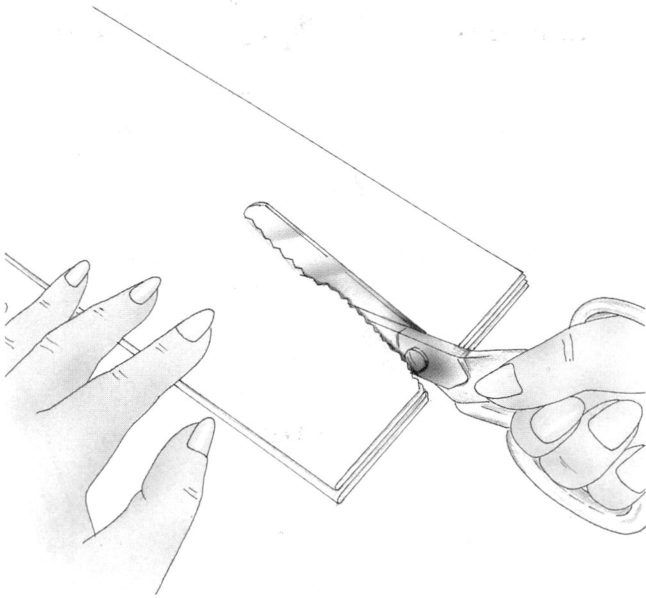

1 TRIMMING THE PAPER
Fold two tissues or napkins in half and lay one on top of the other. Measure 5cm (2in) from the folded edges and cut straight across the folded tissue or napkin with pinking shears. Cut away any patterned border with scissors, then trim the length of the strip to 20cm (7¾in).

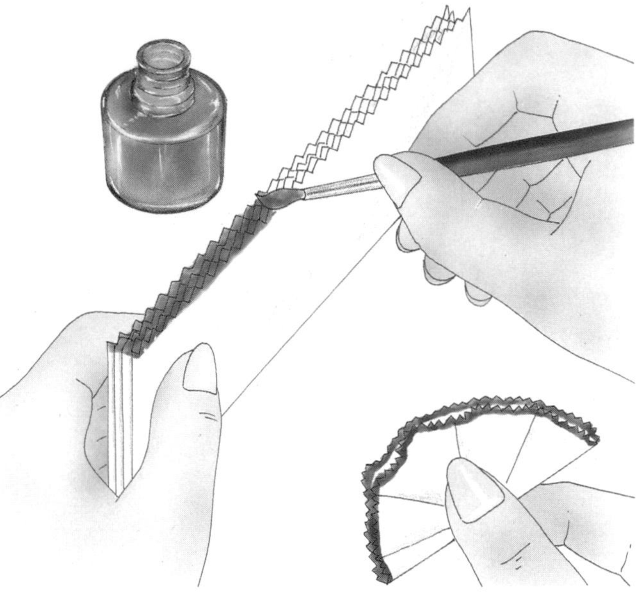

2 PREPARING THE PETALS
Holding the pinked edges of the paper together, paint them lightly with ink, then separate the layers and unfold them. Leave them to dry.

Re-fold each layer and pleat it along the folded edge. Pinch the folded edge to hold the pleats.

3 ATTACHING THE PETALS
Wrap one paper layer around the top of a bamboo cane or garden stick, and wind the binding wire tightly round it. Bind on the remaining petals in the same way.

4 TAPING THE STEM
Wind florists' tape round the base of the petals to hide the binding wire. Continue wrapping the tape down the stem, winding at an angle, and stretching the tape slightly as you work to give a smooth finish.

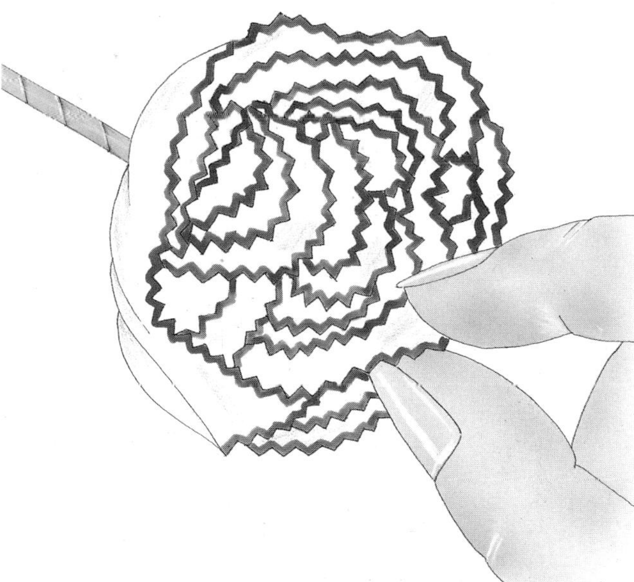

5 ARRANGING THE PETALS
Gently tease apart the petals to shape the flower. Ruffle the surface lightly for a natural look.

Repeat steps 1-5 to make more flowers in different colours, leaving some of them unpainted.

PAPER ASTERS

These pretty asters will flower all year round. Choose realistic colours and make some buds for a natural effect.

MATERIALS

Tissue paper in white, light pink, deep pink, purple, lilac and green

30cm (12in) long split bamboo canes or green garden sticks

Binding wire

12mm (½in) wide leaf green florists' tape

Pinking shears

Scissors

Cotton balls

TEMPLATES

place on a fold

aster leaf

aster bud

Making the Asters

1 MAKING THE PETALS
Cut out four 12 x 25cm (4¾ x 10in) rectangles of coloured tissue. Fold each one in half lengthways and trim 1cm (⅜in) from the long edges with pinking shears. Using scissors, snip into the pinked edges, between the points, to make a 4cm (1⅝in) fringe.

For the green calyx, cut a 10 x 25cm (4 x 10in) rectangle of green tissue and fringe it in the same way.

2 ATTACHING THE PETALS
Pleat the folded edge of each petal and bind it on to one end of the bamboo cane or garden stick with binding wire, as for the PAPER CARNATIONS, step 3. Pleat the green calyx and bind it on in the same way.

3 TAPING THE STEM
Using the leaf template (previous page), cut out three or four leaves from folded green tissue. Wind the florists' tape round the base of the flower and down the stem, inserting the leaves at intervals along the stem. Keep the tape taut so it lies flat.

Making an Aster Bud

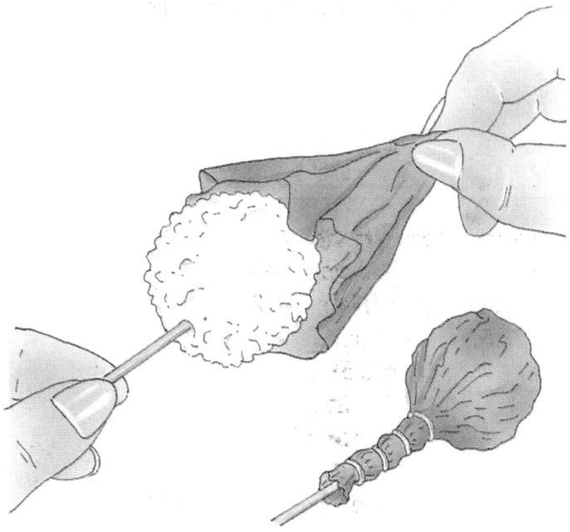

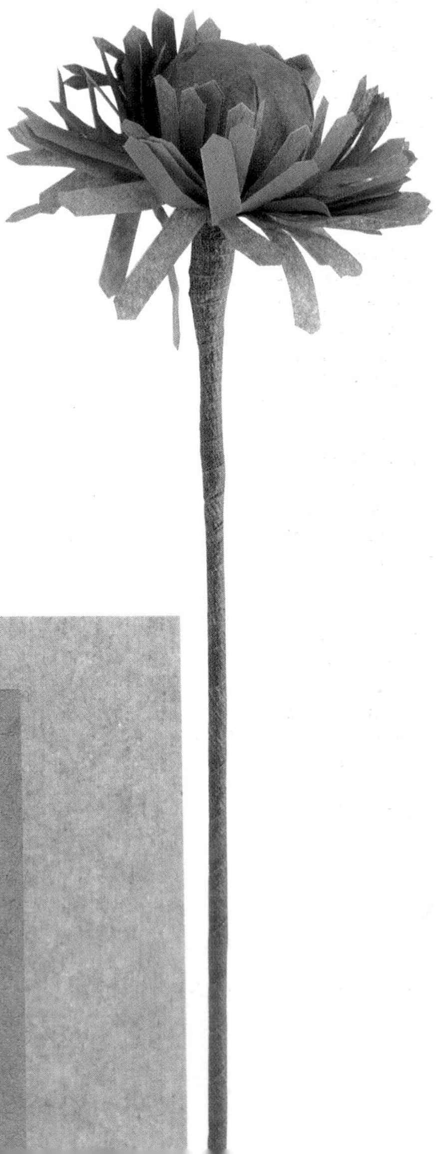

1 COVERING THE CENTRE
Use the aster bud pattern to cut a 10cm (4in) circle from coloured tissue. Stick the end of a bamboo cane or green garden stick into a cotton ball and then wrap the tissue round it, gathering it on to the cane. Bind the tissue to the cane with the wire.

2 FINISHING THE BUD
Make a green calyx and tape it round the bud as in MAKING THE ASTERS, steps 1-2. Cover the stem with florists' tape, inserting leaves if you wish.

INDEX

PICTURE ACKNOWLEDGMENTS

7 Robert Harding Syndication/Homes & Ideas/Christopher Drake, 8(t) Elizabeth Whiting & Associates/Debi Treloar, (b) Robert Harding Syndication/Homes & Gardens/Debi Treloar, 9 Elizabeth Whiting & Associates/Di Lewis, 10(tl) Elizabeth Whiting & Associates/Spike Powell, (tr) Elizabeth Whiting & Associates/Di Lewis, (b) Insight London Picture Library/Michelle Garrett, 11(t) Eaglemoss/Graham Rae, (c) Robert Harding Syndication/IPC Magazines/Ideal Home, (b) Robert Harding Syndication/Homes & Ideas/Dominic Blackmore, 12(t) Robert Harding Syndication/Woman & Home/Jerry Tubby, (bl) Eaglemoss/Graham Rae, (br) Eaglemoss/Paul Bricknell, 13-14 Eaglemoss/Laura Wickenden, 15 Robert Harding Syndication/Homes & Gardens/Trevor Richards, 16(t) Moules, (b) Robert Harding Syndication/Homes & Gardens/Trevor Richards, 17(t) Robert Harding Syndication/Homes & Gardens/Pia Tryde, (b) JahresZeiten/Für Sie/Petra Strange, 18(tl) Robert Harding Syndcation/Woman's Journal/Polly Wreford, (cr) PWA International, (bl) Modes et Travaux, 19 Creative Publishing international, 20(t) Robert Harding Syndication/Homes & Ideas/Andreas von Einsiedel, (b) Creative Publishing international, 21-22 Marie Claire Idées/Becquet/Faure, 23 Eaglemoss/Lizzie Orme, 24 DIY Photo Library, 25(tl) Worldwide Syndication/Wohn Idee, (bl) DIY Photo Library, (br) Eaglemoss/Lizzie Orme, 26 Creative Publishing international, 27-30 Eaglemoss/Gareth Sambidge/Paul Bricknell, 31 Eaglemoss/Lizzie Orme, 32(t, b) Creative Publishing international, (c) Eaglemoss/Lizzie Orme, 33-34 Eaglemoss/Gareth Sambidge, 35 Eaglemoss/Graham Rae, 36-37 Creative Publishing international, 38 Eaglemoss/Graham Rae, 39 Eaglemoss/Steve Tanner, 40 Eaglemoss/Adrian Taylor, 41-42 Eaglemoss/Graham Rae, 42-44 Creative Publishing international, 44(tc) Eaglemoss/Graham Rae, 45-46 Eaglemoss/George Taylor, 47 Robert Harding Syndication/Homes & Gardens/Marie-Louise Avery, 48 Eaglemoss/George Taylor, 49-52 Eaglemoss/Adrian Taylor, 53 Eaglemoss/Martin Chaffer, 54 Eaglemoss/Graham Rae, 55(t) Eaglemoss/Graham Rae, (b) Eaglemoss/Steve Tanner, 56(t) Eaglemoss/Graham Rae, (b) Eaglemoss/Steve Tanner, 57 Eaglemoss/Adrian Taylor, 58 JahresZeiten/Für Sie/Wolfgang Kruger, 59(t) Eaglemoss/Steve Tanner, (b) Eaglemoss/Adrian Taylor, 60 Eaglemoss/Shona Wood, 61-62 Worldwide Syndication, 63-65 Eaglemoss/Adrian Taylor, 66-68 JahresZeiten/Für Sie/Majo Heye, 69 Breslich & Foss, 70(t) Breslich & Foss, (bl) Elizabeth Whiting & Associates/Di Lewis, (br) Eaglemoss/Simon Page-Richie, 71 Ariadne Holland, 72(t,b) Insight London/Michelle Garrett, (c) The Garden Picture Library/Linda Burgess, 73 PWA International, 74(t) PWA International, (c) Worldwide Syndication, (b) Modes et Travaux, 75 The Garden Picture Library/Mayer/LeScaff, 76(t) Elizabeth Whiting & Associates/Di Lewis, (bl)Cent Idées/Maltaverne/Faver, (br) JahresZeiten/ZuHause/Olaf Gollnek, 77 Breslich & Foss, 78(bl) Ariadne Holland, (br) Eaglemoss/Graham Rae, 79(t) Eaglemoss/Graham Rae, (b) Marie Claire Idées/Maltaverne/Faver, 80 Eaglemoss/Steve Tanner, 81 Cent Idées/Duffas/Schoumacher, 82-84 Eaglemoss/Martin Norris, 85-86 Eaglemoss/Graham Rae, 87-88 Eaglemoss/Steve Tanner, 89-90 Eaglemoss/Adrian Taylor, 91 Eaglemoss/Steve Tanner, 92(t) Insight London Picture Library, (c) Breslich & Foss, (b) Eaglemoss/Steve Tanner, 93 Eaglemoss/Steve Tanner, 94(t) Marie Claire Idées/Hussenot /Chastres, (b) Eaglemoss/Steve Tanner, 94-95, PWA International, 95(t) Mulhouse Design, 96(t, bl) Elizabeth Whiting & Associates/Di Lewis, (br) Elizabeth Whiting & Associates/Jerry Tubby, 97 Robert Harding Syndication/Homes & Gardens/James Merrell, 98 Jo Bourne, 99-100 Robert Harding Syndication/IPC Magazines, 101-102 Creative Publishing International, 103 Robert Harding Syndication/IPC Magazines/Homes & Gardens, 104(t) Eaglemoss/Steve Tanner, (c, b) PWA International, 105-108 Robert Harding Syndication/IPC Magazines/Homes & Gardens, 109 Eaglemoss/Graham Rae, 110-112 Eaglemoss/Paul Bricknell/Graham Rae, 113-114 Eaglemoss/Steve Tanner, 115-116 Eaglemoss/Gareth Sambidge/Paul Bricknell, 117-118 Eaglemoss/Adrian Taylor, 119-120 Eaglemoss/Paul Bricknell, 121-122 Modes et Travaux, 123-126 Eaglemoss/Martin Norris.

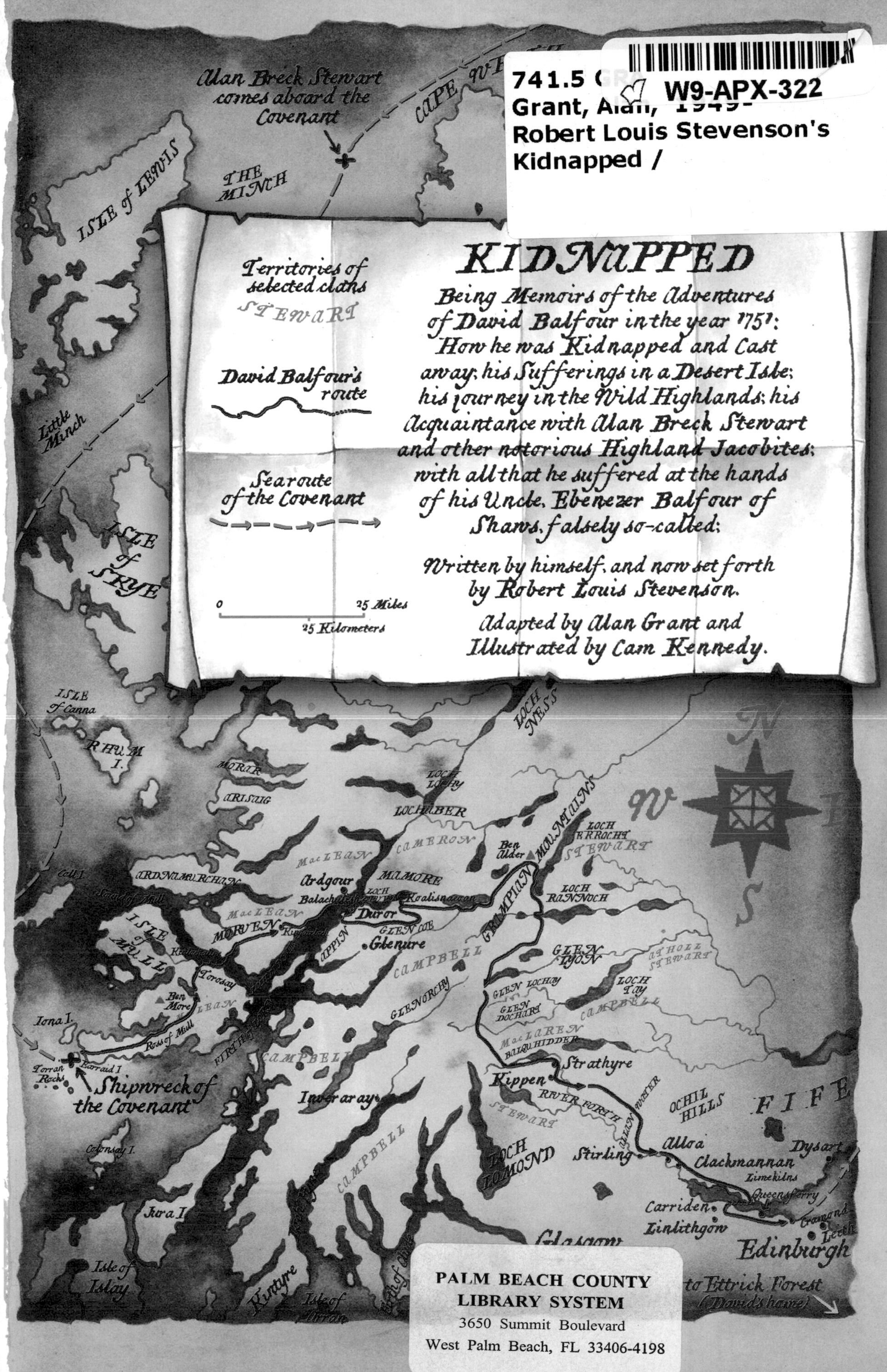
KIDNAPPED
Being Memoirs of the Adventures of David Balfour in the year 1751: How he was Kidnapped and Cast away; his Sufferings in a Desert Isle; his journey in the Wild Highlands; his Acquaintance with Alan Breck Stewart and other notorious Highland Jacobites; with all that he suffered at the hands of his Uncle, Ebenezer Balfour of Shaws, falsely so-called:
Written by himself, and now set forth by Robert Louis Stevenson.
Adapted by Alan Grant and Illustrated by Cam Kennedy.
Territories of selected clans
STEWART
David Balfour's route
Sea route of the Covenant
0
25 Miles
25 Kilometers
Alan Breck Stewart comes aboard the Covenant
CAPE WRATH
THE MINCH
ISLE of LEWIS
Little Minch
ISLE of SKYE
ISLE of Canna
RHUM I.
MORAR
ARISAIG
LOCH NESS
LOCH LOCHY
LOCHABER
CAMERON
Ben Alder
GRAMPIAN MOUNTAINS
LOCH ERROCHT
STEWART
LOCH RANNOCH
ARDNAMURCHAN
MacLEAN
Ardgour
MAMORE
Balachulish
Duror
GLEN COE
APPIN
Glenure
MORVEN
MacLEAN
ISLE of MULL
Torosay
Ben More
LEAN
CAMPBELL
GLEN LYON
ATHOLL STEWART
GLEN LOCHAY
LOCH TAY
GLEN DOCHART
CAMPBELL
GLENORCHY
MacLAREN
BALQUHIDDER
Strathyre
Iona I.
Ross of Mull
Earraid I.
Torran Rocks
Shipwreck of the Covenant
CAMPBELL
Inveraray
Kippen
RIVER FORTH
ALLAN WATER
OCHIL HILLS
FIFE
STEWART
LOCH LOMOND
Stirling
Alloa
Clackmannan
Dysart
Limekilns
Queensferry
Carriden
Linlithgow
Cramond
Leith
Edinburgh
Colonsay I.
CAMPBELL
Jura I.
Glasgow
Isle of Islay
Kintyre
Isle of Arran
to Ettrick Forest (David's home)
N
W
S

On a certain morning in the month of June 1751, I took the key for the last time out of the door of my father's house...
And set out to find my fortune in the wide world.
Mr Campbell, the minister of our village, Essendean, walked with me to the ford...
Before he died, David, your father gave me this letter. You are to deliver it to the House of Shaws.
House of Shaws? What had my poor father to do with such a grand place?
That is where he came from - and it is where he said you should return.
The name of the owner is the same as the name you bear - Ebenezer Balfour.

MY HEART BEAT HARD AT THIS GREAT PROSPECT SUDDENLY OPENING BEFORE A LAD OF SEVENTEEN...

IF YOU WERE IN MY SHOES, SIR, WOULD YOU GO?
THAT WOULD I, AND WITHOUT PAUSE!

THEN I WAS ALONE, OVERJOYED TO GET OUT OF THAT QUIET COUNTRYSIDE, AND GO TO A GREAT, BUSY HOUSE AMONG RICH AND RESPECTED GENTLEFOLK...

I TOOK MY LAST LOOK AT ESSENDEAN, AND THE ROWANS IN THE CHURCHYARD WHERE MY FATHER AND MY MOTHER LAY...

AND SET OUT FOR SHAWS, IN CRAMOND...
TO MEET MY UNKNOWN - AND WEALTHY! - RELATIVE.

ON THE FORENOON OF THE SECOND DAY, COMING TO THE TOP OF A HILL, I SAW ALL THE COUNTRY FALL AWAY BEFORE ME DOWN TO THE SEA; AND IN THE MIDST OF THIS DESCENT, ON A LONG RIDGE, THE CITY OF EDINBURGH SMOKING LIKE A KILN.
THERE WAS A FLAG UPON THE CASTLE, AND SHIPS LYING ANCHORED IN THE FIRTH; BOTH OF WHICH I COULD DISTINGUISH CLEARLY, AND BOTH BROUGHT MY COUNTRY HEART INTO MY MOUTH.

On the Glasgow road I saw some REDCOATS, soldiers of KING GEORGE, who had brutally CRUSHED the HIGHLAND REBELLION only five years earlier...
But when I began to ask after my namesake...
Ye want EBENEZER BALFOUR?
Heed this warning from me, laddie - keep CLEAR of the House of Shaws!
And when I asked a traveling barber what kind of man my uncle might be...
Bah! Nae kind of a man at all!
It was a MYSTERY, all right. And if I hadn't been so FAR from Essendean, I think I might have QUIT my QUEST and gone home again right then and there!

AROUND SUNDOWN I MET A SOUR-LOOKING WOMAN...
THAT IS THE HOUSE OF SHAWS! BLOOD BUILT IT... BLOOD STOPPED THE BUILDING OF IT...
AND BLOOD SHALL BRING IT DOWN!

IF YE SEE THE LAIRD, TELL HIM JENNET CLOUSTON CALLS DOWN A CURSE ON HIM AND HIS HOUSE!
BLACK, BLACK BE THEIR FALL!
I CARRIED MY FATHER'S LETTER, AND I WOULD NOT BE STOPPED. BUT I COULD NOT HELP BUT WONDER: 
WAS THIS THE PALACE I HAD BEEN COMING TO?
WAS IT WITHIN THESE WALLS THAT I WAS TO SEEK NEW FRIENDS AND BEGIN GREAT FORTUNES?

THE LIGHT FROM A FIRE FLICKERED IN THE WINDOWS, BUT AT FIRST MY FRANTIC KNOCKING WENT UNHEEDED...
EBENEZER BALFOUR! I HAVE SOMETHING FOR YOU!

BE OFF WITH YE! THIS BLUNDERBUSS IS LOADED!

I CARRY A LETTER OF INTRODUCTION.
MY NAME IS DAVID BALFOUR.

IS YOUR FATHER DEAD?
AYE, HE'LL BE DEAD, AND THAT'LL BE WHAT BRINGS YE RAPPING ON MY DOOR.

GO INTO THE KITCHEN - AND TOUCH NAETHING!

IT WAS THE BAREST ROOM I EVER SET MY EYES ON. THE TABLE WAS LAID FOR SUPPER WITH A BOWL OF PORRIDGE, A HORN SPOON AND A CUP OF ALE...
GIVE ME ALEXANDER'S LETTER.
YOU KNOW MY FATHER'S NAME?

IT WOULD BE STRANGE IF I DIDNAE. FOR HE WAS MY BROTHER.
SO YOU SEE, DAVIE MY MAN, I AM YOUR BORN UNCLE!

I WAS ASTONISHED, FOR MY FATHER HAD NEVER MENTIONED HE HAD A BROTHER. I SAT AND SUPPED THE MEAGER BOWL OF PORRIDGE HE OFFERED, WHILE HE READ THE LETTER...
YE'LL HAVE HAD SOME HOPES, I'LL WAGER, OF RICH KIN..?
I AM NO BEGGAR. I LOOK FOR NO FAVORS.

NOW LOOK! DINNAE GET HUFFY WITH ME, DAVIE. WE'LL AGREE JUST FINE. NOW COME AWA' TO YOUR BED...

CAN I NOT HAVE A LIGHT, UNCLE?
LIGHTS IN A HOUSE IS A THING I DINNAE AGREE WITH, DAVIE. I'M A-FEARED OF FIRES, YE SEE.

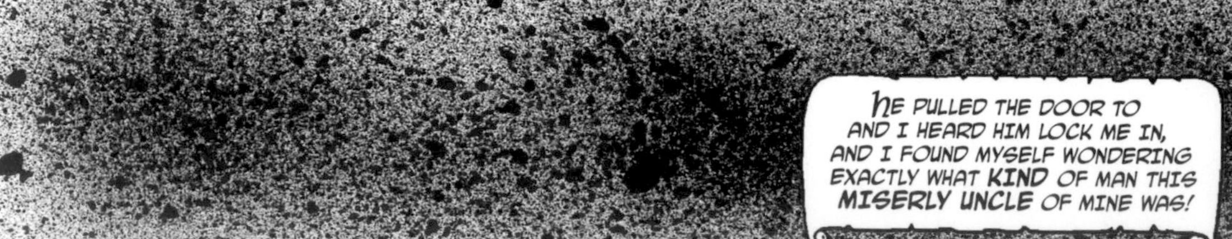
HE PULLED THE DOOR TO AND I HEARD HIM LOCK ME IN, AND I FOUND MYSELF WONDERING EXACTLY WHAT KIND OF MAN THIS MISERLY UNCLE OF MINE WAS!

By the light of the **DAWN**, I saw that ten, or perhaps twenty years ago, this must have been as **PLEASANT** a room as a man could wish.
But time, and severe neglect, had done their worst.

My uncle's diet seemed to consist only of porridge and weak beer...
It is obvious you do not want me here, sir. Family or not, it might be better if I leave.
No, no. Easy Davie, easy! Just wait a day or two ... I'll do the right thing by you, you'll see.

I passed some time in the old library...

Where I made a discovery that troubled me...
My father was supposed to be the **YOUNGER** child...
To my brother Ebenezer on his fifth birthday
So how could he write so **WELL**?

When I asked my uncle about it...
Were you and my father **TWINS**, by any chance?
Eh? **EH?**

WHY DO YE ASK ME THAT?
WHY? EH? EH?
TAKE YOUR HANDS OFF ME, SIR. THIS IS NO WAY TO BEHAVE!
YE SHOULDNAE SPEAK TO ME ABOUT YOUR FATHER, DAVIE. THAT'S WHERE THE MISTAKE IS.
HE WAS THE ONLY BROTHER I EVER HAD!
I BEGAN TO WONDER IF MY UNCLE WAS PERHAPS INSANE, AND EVEN DANGEROUS. BUT ALSO, A SUSPICION BEGAN TO GROW...
ABOUT A POOR LAD WHO WAS A RIGHTFUL HEIR... AND A WICKED UNCLE THAT TRIED TO KEEP HIM FROM HIS INHERITANCE.
WHAT THE MISER DID NEXT THREW ME INTO COMPLETE CONFUSION...
THIS IS FOR YOU, DAVID. FORTY POUNDS IN GOLD COIN!
I'M A QUEER MAN, AND STRANGE WI' STRANGERS, BUT I'LL ALWAYS DO RIGHT BY MY BROTHER'S SON!
NOW YOU DO SOMETHING FOR ME. THIS IS THE KEY FOR THE STAIR TOWER. RIGHT AT THE TOP THERE'S A CHEST WI' PAPERS IN IT. BRING THAT CHEST TAE ME!

THE NIGHT WAS BLACK AND A **STORM** WAS BREWING...
THE TOWER STAIRS WERE **STEEP**, WITH NO **BANNISTER**. I STAYED CLOSE TO THE WALL, ASCENDING SLOWLY...
A BLINK OF **LIGHTNING** CAME AND WENT - AND IF I DID NOT CRY OUT, IT WAS BECAUSE **FEAR** HAD ME BY THE **THROAT**!
I AM MERE INCHES FROM DISASTER!
I GOT DOWN ON MY HANDS AND KNEES AND CRAWLED ON, FENDING OFF THE GREAT STIR OF **BATS** THAT FLITTERED IN THE TOP PART OF THE TOWER.

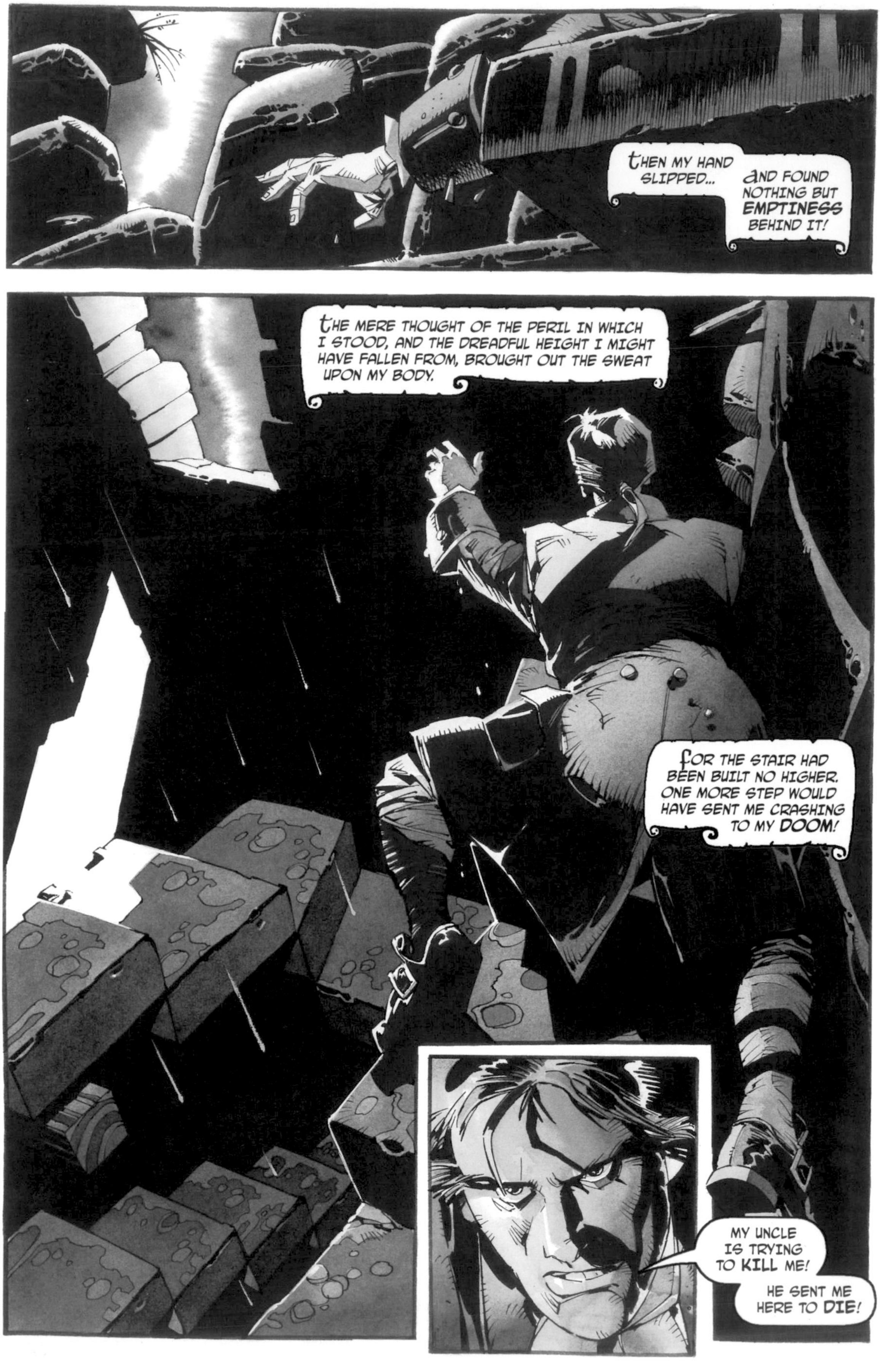

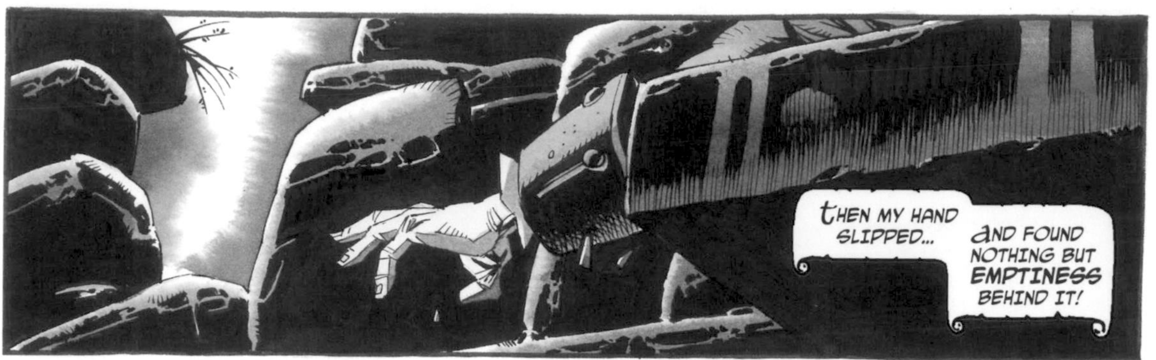

THE MERE THOUGHT OF THE PERIL IN WHICH I STOOD, AND THE DREADFUL HEIGHT I MIGHT HAVE FALLEN FROM, BROUGHT OUT THE SWEAT UPON MY BODY.

FOR THE STAIR HAD BEEN BUILT NO HIGHER. ONE MORE STEP WOULD HAVE SENT ME CRASHING TO MY **DOOM**!

MY UNCLE IS TRYING TO **KILL** ME!

HE SENT ME HERE TO **DIE**!

ANGER BURNED IN MY HEART AS I GROPED MY WAY DOWN. BY THE TIME I REACHED GROUND, THE STORM HAD BROKEN...
THERE HE IS - LISTENING FOR THE SOUND OF MY FALL!

THERE WAS A GREAT TOW-ROW OF THUNDER. MY UNCLE WAS SEIZED BY A KIND OF PANIC FEAR AND RAN INSIDE...

I CAME CLOSE BEHIND HIM, AND SUDDENLY CLAPPED MY HANDS UPON HIS SHOULDERS...
AH-HA!
AIIEEEE!

D-D-DAVIE! ARE YE ALIVE? O, MAN, ARE YE ALIVE?
THAT I AM... SMALL THANKS TO YOU!

WHY GIVE ME MONEY - THEN TRY TO KILL ME? WHY DO YOU FEAR ME SO?
I-I'LL TELL YE EVERYTHING, DAVIE. IN THE MORNING.
IT'S MY HEART, YE SEE. I'M FEELING VERY WEAK!

I LOCKED HIM IN HIS ROOM, AND MADE UP SUCH A BLAZE AS HAD NOT SHONE IN THAT KITCHEN FOR MANY A LONG YEAR.
DEEP INTO THE NIGHT, I SAT THERE, AND PONDERED ON THE MYSTERY OF THIS RUINED HOUSE OF SHAWS.

NEXT MORNING, I URGED HIM TO ANSWER ME. BUT...
COME NOW, DAVIE! LET ME FINISH MY PARRITCH!

HIS ATTEMPTS TO THINK UP SOME CUNNING LIE WERE INTERRUPTED BY A KNOCKING AT THE DOOR...
YOU STAY WHERE YOU ARE, SIR. I WILL SEE TO IT.

WHAT CHEER, MATE?
I'VE BROUGHT A LETTER FROM OLD HEASY-OASY TO MR BELFLOWER.
AN' I SAY, MATE - I'M HUNGRY.
MORTAL HUNGRY!

LISTEN TO THIS, DAVIE!
MY PARTNER, CAPTAIN HOSEASON, REQUIRES MY PRESENCE AT THE QUEEN'S FERRY.
IF YE COME WITH ME, WE CAN VISIT WITH THE LAWYER, RANKEILLOR. HE WAS A FRIEND OF YOUR FATHER'S.

MY UNCLE WOULD HARDLY DARE VIOLENCE AGAINST ME AT A BUSY HARBOR. AND I WAS EAGER TO MEET A MAN OF THE LAW, MOREOVER ONE WHO KNEW MY FATHER...
VERY WELL.
LET US GO!

THEY CALLS ME **RANSOME,** MATE.
I BEEN A SALTY SEA-DOG SINCE I WERE ONLY A LITTL'UN.

CAPTAIN HEASY-OASY'S A HARD MAN, BUT HE AIN'T NO SAILOR. MR **SHUAN'S** CHIEF MATE, AN' HE SAILS THE BOAT.
BUT WHEN HE'S **DRUNK,** HE **BEATS** ME SOMETHIN' AWFUL!

HE'LL BE **SORRY** ONE DAY, YOU SEE IF HE AIN'T!
I'VE KILLED A MAN AFORE, YE KNOW. AYE, **MORE** THAN ONE!

BUT THERE'S WORSE OFF THAN ME.
THERE'S THE **TWENTY-POUNDERS** - MEN **KIDNAPPED** TO BE SOLD AS **SLAVES** IN THE COTTON FIELDS OF **AMERICA!**

THE LAD WAS HALF-CRAZED, AND HIS SHIP - A BRIG CALLED THE COVENANT - SOUNDED A NIGHTMARE ON THE HIGH SEAS.
I WAS GLAD WHEN WE REACHED THE INN.
FOOLISHLY... AS IT WOULD TRANSPIRE... I LEFT MY UNCLE AND THE CAPTAIN TO THEIR BUSINESS, WHILE I EXPLORED THE HARBOR...
SOME SAILORS WAITED IN THE SKIFF FOR THEIR CAPTAIN, AND A MORE DESPERATE AND UNSAVORY LOT I HAD NEVER BEFORE SEEN...
I SUPPED SOME ALE AND CONVERSED WITH THE LANDLORD...
EBENEZER BALFOUR IS A WICKED AULD MAN, SIR!
THERE'S MANY WOULD LIKE TO SEE HIM BROUGHT LOW - LIKE JENNET CLOUSTON, WHO HE EVICTED FROM HER OWN HAME!
THEY SAY EBENEZER KILLED HIS BROTHER!
NO, HE DIDN'T. BUT WHY WOULD HE, ANYWAY?
TO GET HIS HANDS ON THE HOUSE OF SHAWS!
YOU MEAN - ALEXANDER WAS THE ELDEST SON? HE SHOULD HAVE INHERITED THE HOUSE?
AND THAT EXPLAINED EVERYTHING. MY UNCLE HAD CHEATED MY FATHER - HIS OWN BROTHER! - IN ORDER TO LAY HANDS ON SHAWS!
THAT RUINED HOUSE, AND ALL ITS LANDS, WAS REALLY MINE!

SHORTLY, CAPTAIN HOSEASON HIMSELF CAME TO SEE ME...
YOUR UNCLE TELLS ME GREAT THINGS OF YOU, DAVID. YE SHALL COME ON BOARD MY SHIP, AND DRINK A BOWL.
I AM SORRY, CAPTAIN. BUT I MUST SEE RANKEILLOR, THE LAWYER.

TAKE CARE, LAD. YOUR UNCLE MEANS TO DO YOU HARM!
COME ABOARD MY BOAT UNTIL I CAN HAVE A PRIVATE WORD WITH YOU!

I THOUGHT I HAD FOUND A FRIEND, SOMEONE WHO WOULD HELP ME IN MY DIFFICULTY.

SO, LIKE A FOOL, I WENT WILLINGLY TO MY FATE...

THE CAPTAIN AND I WERE FIRST TO BE HOIST ABOARD...

BUT WHERE IS MY UNCLE?

AYE, LAD. THAT'S THE POINT!

THE SKIFF WAS HEADING BACK TO SHORE...
I'VE BEEN TRICKED!

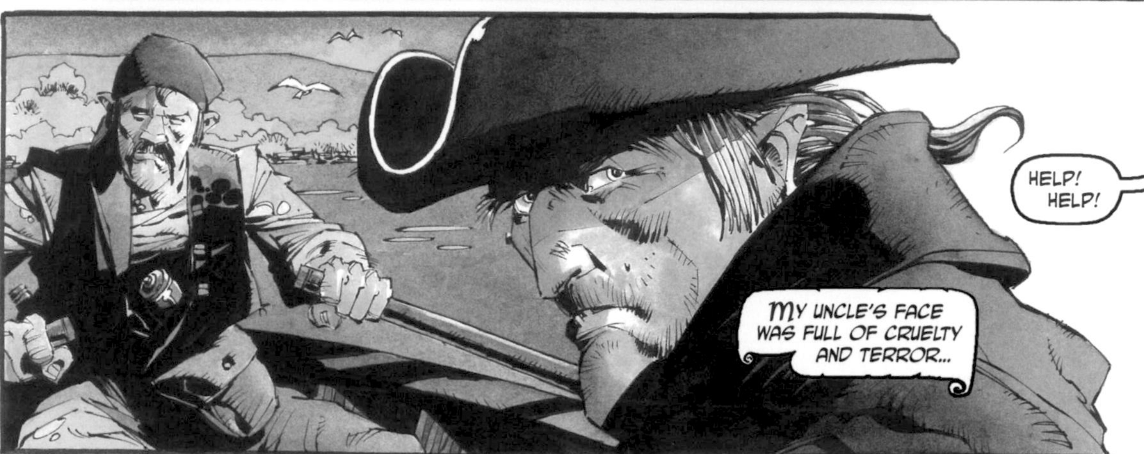
HELP! HELP!
MY UNCLE'S FACE WAS FULL OF CRUELTY AND TERROR...

STRONG HANDS GRABBED ME AND PULLED ME AWAY...

I SAW A GREAT FLASH OF FIRE AS A THUNDERBOLT SEEMED TO STRIKE ME...

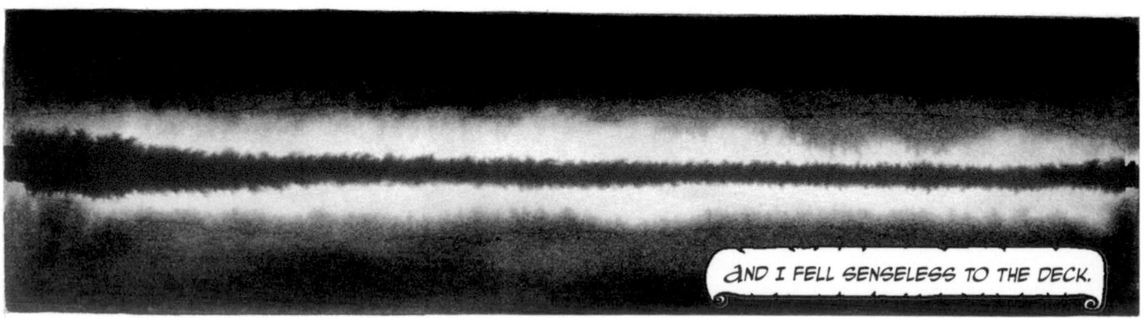
AND I FELL SENSELESS TO THE DECK.

I CAME TO IN DARKNESS, IN GREAT PAIN. THE WHOLE WORLD HEAVED GIDDILY UP AND DOWN, AND I HEARD THE ROARING OF WATER AND THE SHRILL CRIES OF SEAMEN...

IT TOOK ME A LONG WHILE TO REALIZE I MUST BE LYING SOMEWHERE IN THE BELLY OF THAT UNLUCKY SHIP, AND THAT WE WERE PLOWING THROUGH A GALE.
THERE FELL ON ME A BLACKNESS OF DESPAIR, A HORROR OF REMORSE AT MY OWN FOLLY, AND A PASSION OF ANGER AT MY TRAITOROUS UNCLE.

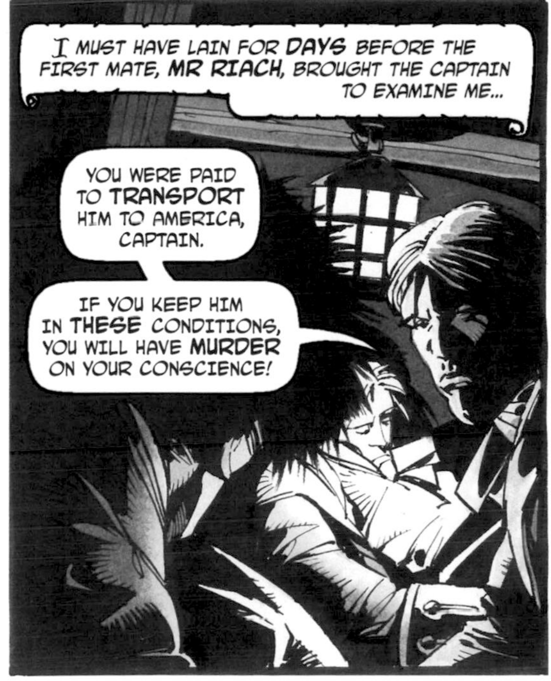
I MUST HAVE LAIN FOR DAYS BEFORE THE FIRST MATE, MR RIACH, BROUGHT THE CAPTAIN TO EXAMINE ME...
YOU WERE PAID TO TRANSPORT HIM TO AMERICA, CAPTAIN.
IF YOU KEEP HIM IN THESE CONDITIONS, YOU WILL HAVE MURDER ON YOUR CONSCIENCE!

I WAS PUT IN THE FORECASTLE WITH THE OTHER MEN, AND HERE I STAYED RECOVERING.
THEY WERE A ROUGH LOT, AS SAILORS MOSTLY ARE. SOME AMONG THEM HAD SAILED WITH PIRATES, WHILE OTHERS WERE DESERTERS FROM KING GEORGE'S NAVY.

But, for the most part, they were not evil... with the exception perhaps of the drunken MR SHUAN...
Ye scurvy brat! Ye deserve a good wollopin'!

But Shuan was the only TRUE SAILOR amongst the whole lot.
They NEEDED his knowledge, and so none would be critical.

I tried to befriend Ransome, but truth be told, his mind was scarcely human...
Oh 'tis my delight on a shiny night in the season of the year!

Don't remember me father. He made clocks, I fink. We had a STARLIN', see, that could whistle right pretty.
Don't you want to FIND your father? To go HOME?

THIS be my home now. The SEA, an' the WIND, an' me pannikin of ALE!

All this time, the ship was meeting constant headwinds and rough sea, meaning hard labor for all hands.

THEN ONE DAY...
AHOY, MATEY!
PANNIKIN OF ALE FOR MR SHUAN, SIR!
YOU PEA-BRAINED BRAT! IT'S FILTHY!
LET THAT BE A LESSON TO YE!
HE - HE'S DEAD! YOU SOT AND SWINE, SHUAN! YOU'VE KILLED HIM!
THE STORY IS - IT WAS AN ACCIDENT. RANSOME WAS DRUNK, AND HE FELL OVERBOARD. DON'T FORGET IT!
AS FOR YOU, DAVID BALFOUR - YOU WILL BE CABIN BOY!

MORE THAN A WEEK WENT BY, AND MY HEART SANK LOWER AND LOWER.
THE SHADOW OF POOR RANSOME LAY HEAVILY ON ME, AND STILL I WAS BOUND FOR SLAVERY. EVEN THE SHIP ITSELF SEEMED CURSED WITH ILL LUCK...

ON THE TENTH NIGHT THERE WAS A TERRIBLE SHRIEK OF TORTURED WOOD AND THE SOUND OF DESPERATE CRIES...
FOR PITY'S SAKE! THEY'VE RUN US DOWN!

THERE'S A SURVIVOR!
THROW HIM A LINE AND WE'LL SAVE HIM YET!

He was SMALLISH in stature, but well-set and NIMBLE as a goat. His face was pitted with the SMALLPOX, and his EYES had a kind of dancing MADNESS in them...
I AM A JACOBITE, SIR - ONE OF THOSE WHO REBELLED AGAINST THE ENGLISH KING IN 'FORTY-FIVE.
A man I would rather call my FRIEND than my ENEMY...
IF I SHOULD FALL INTO THE HANDS OF THE REDCOATS, IT WILL GO HARD FOR ME!
After their rebellion was CRUSHED, many of the HIGHLAND CHIEFS fled to FRANCE. They sent back men such as this one, to collect their RENTS from the CLAN MEMBERS and deliver the money abroad.
I AM A WHIG, SIR, AND LOYAL TO THE KING. BUT FOR SIXTY OF THOSE GOLDEN GUINEAS, I WILL SAIL YOU TO LOCH LINNHE!
THEN HERE'S MY HAND UPON IT!

THE CAPTAIN WENT OUT - HURRIEDLY, I THOUGHT - AND LEFT ME ALONE WITH THE STRANGER...
SO...YOU ARE A REBEL, SIR?
AYE. AND YOU, BY YOUR LONG FACE, ARE A WHIG.

WELL, MR WHIG - THIS BOTTLE IS DRY.
IT'S NOT EASY TO PAY SIXTY GUINEAS, AND BE GRUDGED A WEE DRAM!
I WILL ASK THE CAPTAIN FOR MORE.

I HEARD MUFFLED VOICES IN THE FOG...
WE CAN FALL ONE UPON EACH SIDE OF HIM, AND PIN HIM BY THE ARMS!
WE CAN STAB HIM BEFORE HE HAS TIME TO DRAW!

DAVID! YON WILD HIELANDMAN IS A DANGER TO THE SHIP AND AN ENEMY OF OUR KING!
YOU MUST GET US THE FIREARMS FROM THE ROUND-HOUSE... AND WE WILL SHARE HIS GOLD WITH YOU!

VERY WELL, SIRS.
I WILL DO IT.
BUT I WAS SEIZED WITH ANGER AT THESE TREACHEROUS, GREEDY, BLOODY MEN - AND I KNEW I COULD NOT DO IT!

DO YE WANT TO BE KILLED, JACOBITE?
EH?
WHAT'S THIS YE SAY?
THEY'RE ALL MURDERERS HERE! THEY'VE KILLED A BOY ALREADY - AND NOW IT'S YOU!

AYE, AYE... BUT THEY HAVEN'T GOT ME YET.
WILL YE STAND WITH ME, LAD?
I AM NO THIEF, NOR YET MURDERER! I'LL STAND BY YOU. I AM DAVID BALFOUR.
OF SHAWS.

MY NAME IS STEWART A KING'S NAME. BUT THEY CALL ME ALAN BRECK.

WE DOLED OUT CUTLASSES AND PISTOLS FROM THE STORE...
THERE ARE FIFTEEN AGAINST US!
I WILL GUARD THE MAIN DOOR, DAVID. YOU MUST TAKE THE REST!

I WARN YOU, ALAN BRECK - I AM NO GREAT SHOT!
THEN DINNAE FIRE TO THIS SIDE - FOR I WOULD RATHER HAVE TEN FOES IN FRONT OF ME, THAN ONE FRIEND LIKE YOU CRACKING PISTOLS AT MY BACK!

It came all of a sudden, with a rush of feet and a roar...
A golden guinea for every man! Show them no mercy!

That's him that killed the boy!
Just you look to your window, David!

Alan's warning came none too soon...
Smash down that door!

TAKE THAT!
I HAD NEVER FIRED A PISTOL IN MY LIFE, BUT IT WAS NOW OR NEVER...

THEY BROKE AND RAN...

WHILE INSIDE, ALAN BRECK'S SWORD RAN RED WITH BLOOD.

I WOUNDED AT LEAST ONE OF THEM!
AND I HAVE SETTLED TWO.
BUT THAT'S NOT ENOUGH BLOOD, DAVID BALFOUR...

THIS WAS BUT A DRAM BEFORE THE MEAT.
THEY WILL BE BACK IN FORCE!

A SINGLE CALL ON THE SEA-PIPE WAS THEIR SIGNAL. A KNOT OF THEM MADE A RUSH OF IT, CUTLASS IN HAND, AGAINST THE DOOR.
AT THE SAME MOMENT, THE GLASS OF THE SKYLIGHT WAS DASHED IN A THOUSAND PIECES AS A MAN LEAPED THROUGH...

NOW YE'LL DIE, YE...
AAAGH!

A SECOND ASSAILANT TRIED TO LEAP UPON ME...
HAVE THAT FOR YOUR TROUBLE!

THEN I SNATCHED UP MY CUTLASS AND HURRIED TO AID ALAN BRECK STEWART...
AAAH! AGH!

OUR ATTACKERS BROKE BEFORE HIM LIKE WATER, AS THE SWORD IN HIS HANDS FLASHED LIKE QUICKSILVER INTO THEIR MASS...
AND AT EVERY FLASH, THERE CAME THE SCREAM OF A MAN HURT.

ALAN CAME UP TO ME WITH OPEN ARMS, AND EMBRACED ME...
DAVID, LAD - I LOVE YE LIKE A BROTHER!
AND O, MAN, AM I NO' A BONNIE FIGHTER?
MR SHUAN AND FIVE MORE WERE KILLED OUTRIGHT, AND FOUR MORE WERE HURT...
ALL OF A SUDDEN, I BEGAN TO CRY LIKE ANY CHILD...
HUSH, DAVID. YE ARE A BRAW LAD. IT TAKES MUCH TO KILL A MAN, FOR IT GOES AGAINST HUMAN NATURE!
I HAD THESE BUTTONS FROM MY FATHER, DUNCAN.
I GIVE ONE OF THEM TO YOU, DAVID, A KEEPSAKE FOR THIS NIGHT'S BLOODY WORK.
WHEREVER YE GO AND SHOW THAT BUTTON, THE FRIENDS OF ALAN BRECK WILL COME TO AID YOU!

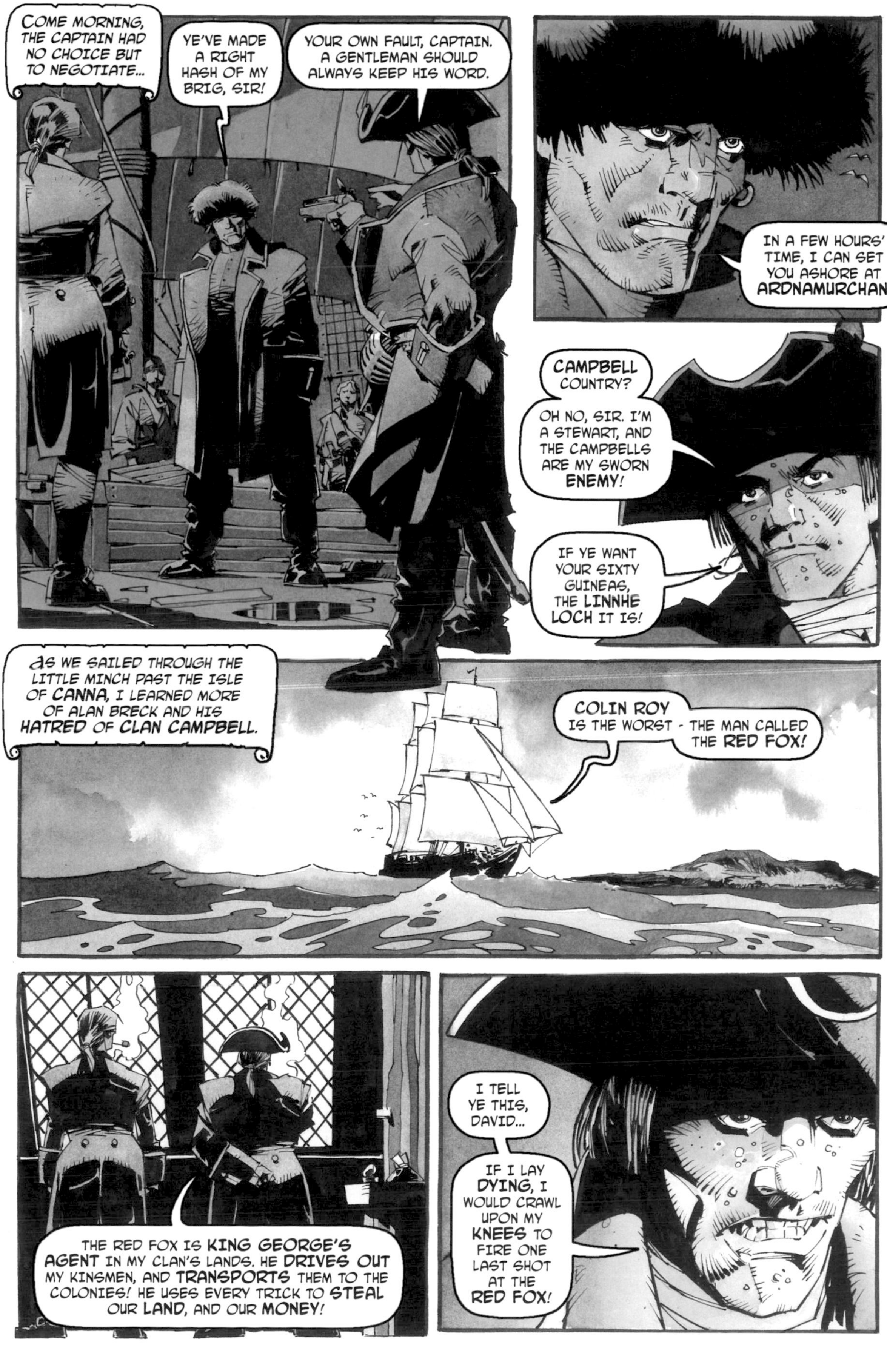

COME MORNING, THE CAPTAIN HAD NO CHOICE BUT TO NEGOTIATE...
YE'VE MADE A RIGHT HASH OF MY BRIG, SIR!
YOUR OWN FAULT, CAPTAIN. A GENTLEMAN SHOULD ALWAYS KEEP HIS WORD.
IN A FEW HOURS' TIME, I CAN SET YOU ASHORE AT **ARDNAMURCHAN**.
CAMPBELL COUNTRY?
OH NO, SIR. I'M A STEWART, AND THE CAMPBELLS ARE MY SWORN **ENEMY**!
IF YE WANT YOUR SIXTY GUINEAS, THE **LINNHE LOCH** IT IS!
AS WE SAILED THROUGH THE LITTLE MINCH PAST THE ISLE OF **CANNA**, I LEARNED MORE OF ALAN BRECK AND HIS **HATRED** OF **CLAN CAMPBELL**.
COLIN ROY IS THE WORST - THE MAN CALLED THE **RED FOX**!

At daybreak I climbed a rugged hill. There was no sign of the brig, or the skiff, and in what I could see of the land was neither house nor man.

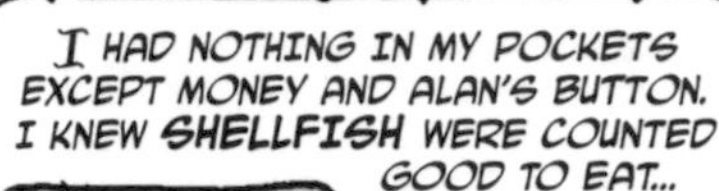
I had nothing in my pockets except money and Alan's button. I knew **shellfish** were counted good to eat...

Perhaps those I gathered were out of season...

When a **guinea** fell from my pocket, my hopes were dashed further. I had left the shore at Queensferry with close on **fifty pounds** in my pocket...

I had little over **three pounds** left - and me the rightful heir of an estate, now **starving** on an isle at the extreme end of the wild Highlands!

Once, a fishers' boat passed by...
Help!
In the name of God have pity! Please - help me!
But they only laughed fit to burst, as if my plight was for them mere entertainment...
I was four days in that God-forsaken place before I found out why they laughed.
The islet was tidal.
At low tide, I could wade across to Mull!
I have seen wicked men and fools, a great many of both - and I believe they both get paid in the end.
But the fools get paid first!

About five or six at night, I came upon a house...
And in answer to my fervent questions...
AYE, I'VE HAD SHIPWRECKED SAILORS HERE.
BUT FIRST THERE WAS A MAN THAT CAME ALONE - ALL DRESSED IN HIS FINERY.
SO ALAN IS STILL ALIVE!
ARE YOU THE LAD WI' THE SILLER BUTTON?
WHY, YES I AM! SEE - HERE IT IS!
THEN I HAVE A MESSAGE FOR YOU.
YOU ARE TO FOLLOW HIM TO HIS OWN LANDS, TO THE PLACE CALLED TOROSAY!
The Highland dress - the KILT - had been FORBIDDEN by law since the rebellion, to try and break the clan spirit. But it was POVERTY that had broken the people I saw.

NEXT MORNING...
WHICH WAY TO TOROSAY, MY FRIEND?
NAE ENGLISH! GO AWAY! NAE ENGLISH!

SO I LET MY MONEY SPEAK FOR ME...

AND SUDDENLY, HE FOUND HIS TONGUE...
TOROSAY?
OCH AYE, IT'S NO' SAE FAR AT ALL, AT ALL. I'LL JUST TAK' YE THERE MYSEL', AND IT'LL ONLY COST YE FIVE SHILLINGS!

WE WALKED FOR MILES IN SILENCE, UNTIL...
I'LL BE NEEDING FIVE SHILLINGS MORE NOO - OR YE CAN FIND YER AIN WAY!
WHY, YOU IMPUDENT, CHEATING RUFFIAN!

YE'LL PAY UP, BY HOOK OR BY CROOK!

BUT I WAS A STRONG LAD, AND VERY ANGRY...

PERHAPS, SIR, THAT WILL TEACH YOU TO KEEP YOUR WORD IN THE FUTURE!

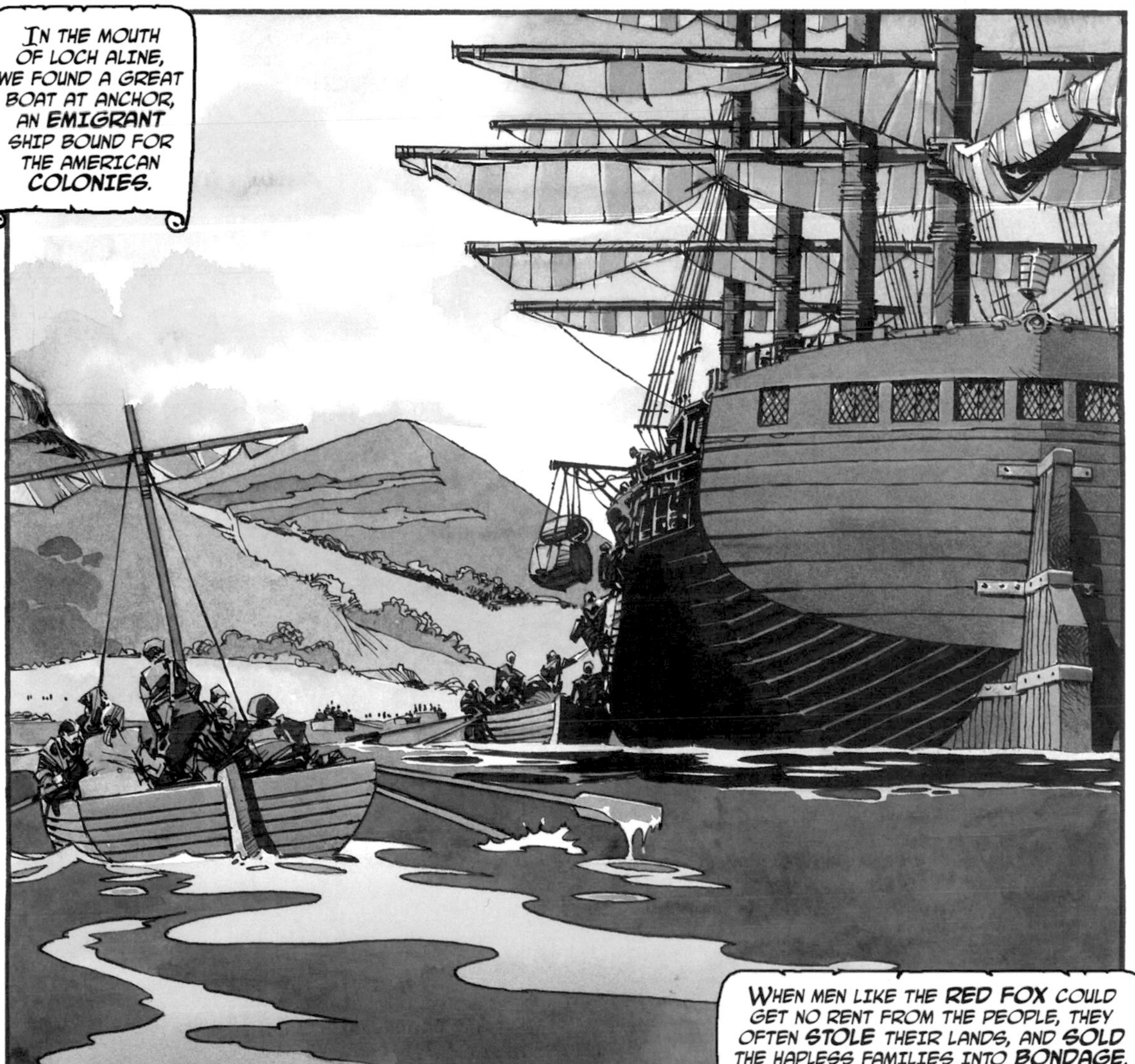

IN THE MOUTH OF LOCH ALINE, WE FOUND A GREAT BOAT AT ANCHOR, AN **EMIGRANT** SHIP BOUND FOR THE AMERICAN **COLONIES**.

WHEN MEN LIKE THE **RED FOX** COULD GET NO RENT FROM THE PEOPLE, THEY OFTEN **STOLE** THEIR LANDS, AND **SOLD** THE HAPLESS FAMILIES INTO **BONDAGE**.

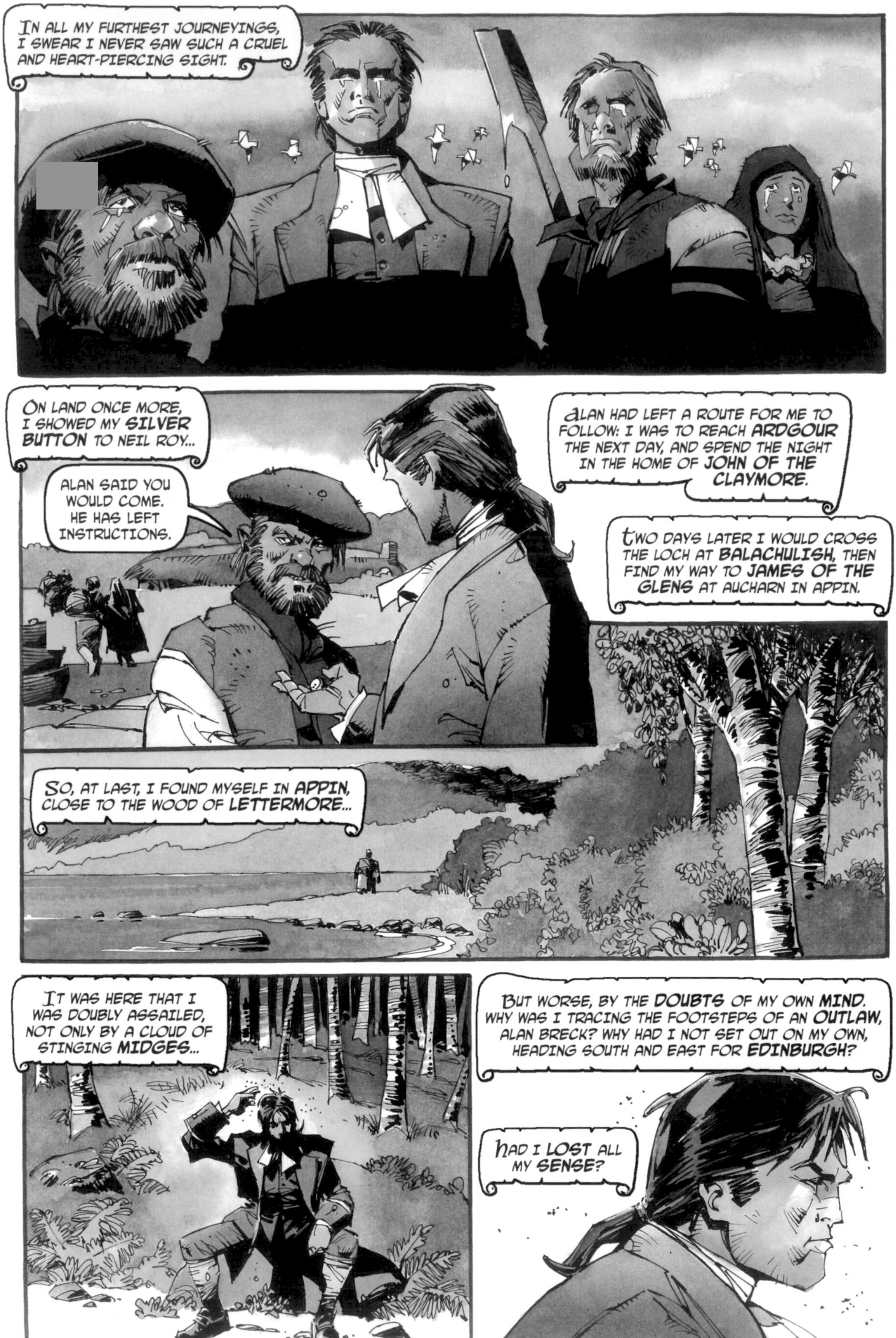

In all my furthest journeyings, I swear I never saw such a cruel and heart-piercing sight.

On land once more, I showed my **silver button** to Neil Roy...

Alan said you would come. He has left instructions.

Alan had left a route for me to follow: I was to reach **Ardgour** the next day, and spend the night in the home of **John of the Claymore**.

Two days later I would cross the loch at **Balachulish**, then find my way to **James of the Glens** at Aucharn in Appin.

So, at last, I found myself in **Appin**, close to the wood of **Lettermore**...

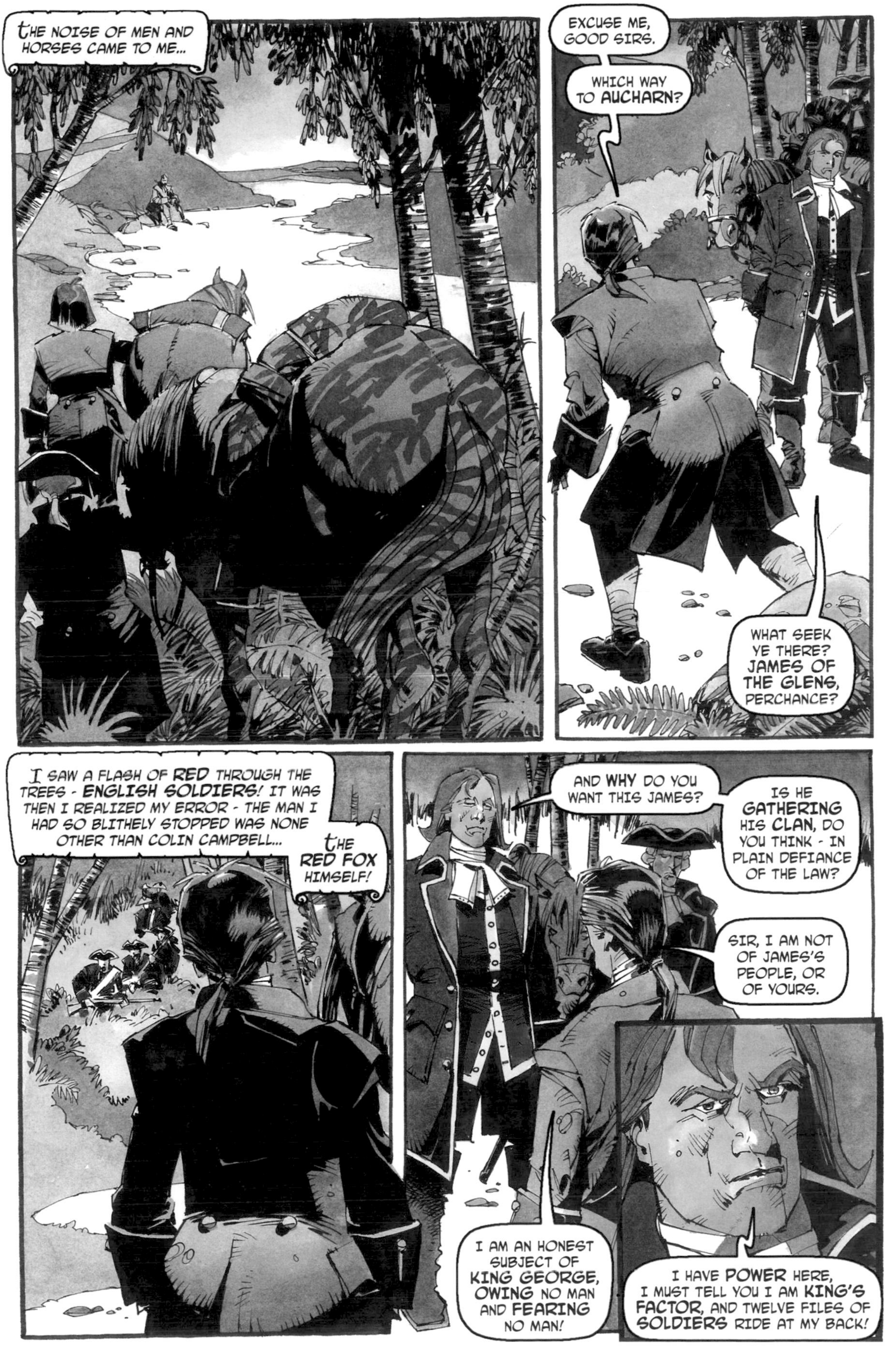

I SAW A FLASH OF RED THROUGH THE TREES - ENGLISH SOLDIERS! IT WAS THEN I REALIZED MY ERROR - THE MAN I HAD SO BLITHELY STOPPED WAS NONE OTHER THAN COLIN CAMPBELL...

THE RED FOX HIMSELF!

AND WHY DO YOU WANT THIS JAMES?

IS HE GATHERING HIS CLAN, DO YOU THINK - IN PLAIN DEFIANCE OF THE LAW?

SIR, I AM NOT OF JAMES'S PEOPLE, OR OF YOURS.

I AM AN HONEST SUBJECT OF KING GEORGE, OWING NO MAN AND FEARING NO MAN!

I HAVE POWER HERE, I MUST TELL YOU I AM KING'S FACTOR, AND TWELVE FILES OF SOLDIERS RIDE AT MY BACK!

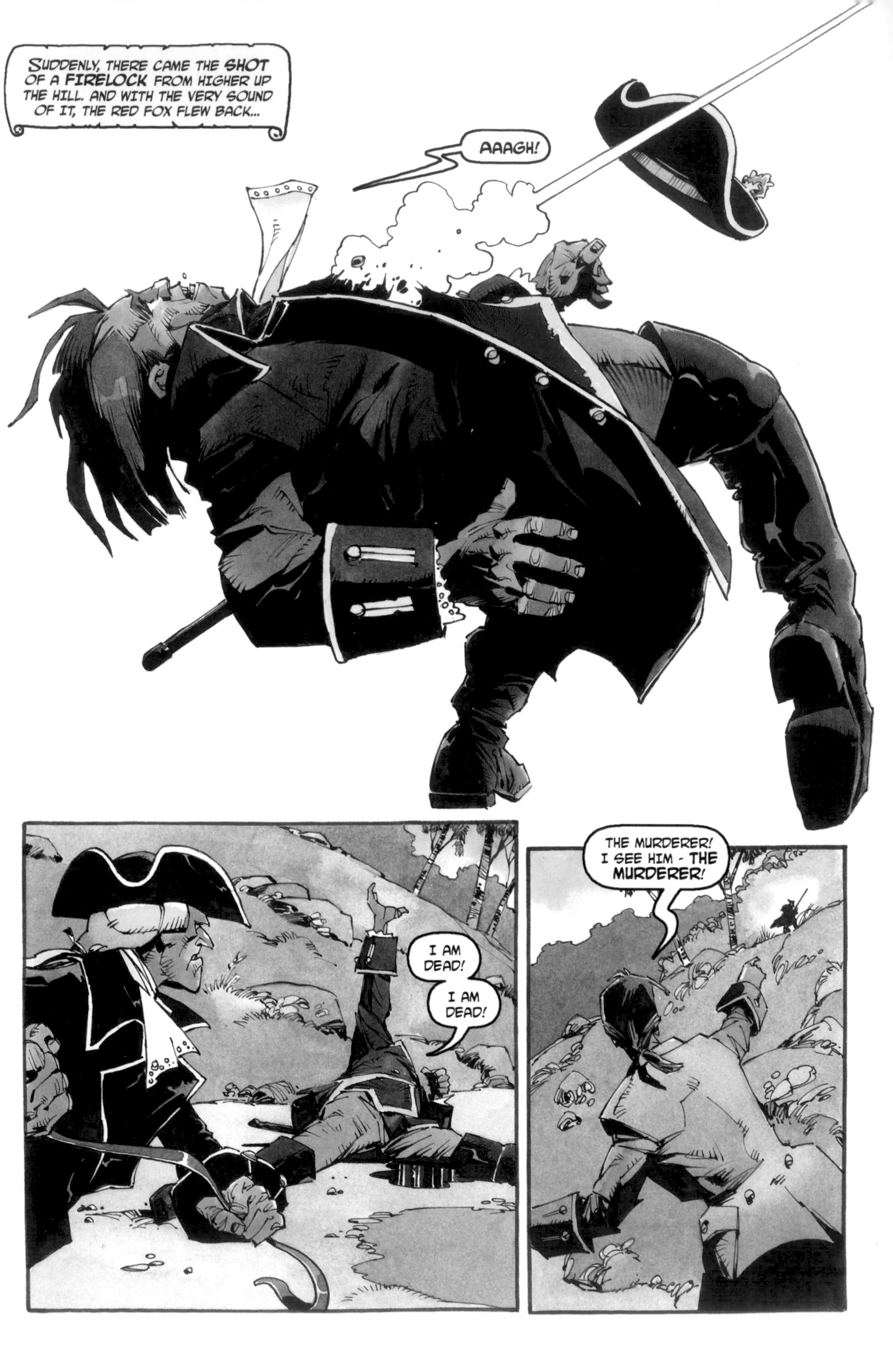

SUDDENLY, THERE CAME THE **SHOT** OF A **FIRELOCK** FROM HIGHER UP THE HILL. AND WITH THE VERY SOUND OF IT, THE RED FOX FLEW BACK...

AAAGH!

HURRY! WE CAN CATCH HIM YET!

THAT LAD IS AN ACCOMPLICE! TEN POUNDS TO THE MAN WHO SHOOTS HIM DEAD!

FIRELOCKS BANGED, AND THE BALLS WHISTLED IN THE BIRCHES, AND MY HEART CAME INTO MY MOUTH WITH TERROR.

THIS WAS NOT THE WAY IT SHOULD BE!

YOU HEARD THE LAWYER. TEN POUNDS FOR HIS LIFE!

I RAN FOR ALL I WAS WORTH...

UNTIL, MOST ASTONISHINGLY, I HEARD A VOICE...
DODGE IN HERE AMONG THE BUSHES!

ALAN! ALAN BRECK!
IT IS NO TIME FOR CIVILITIES, DAVIE.
FOR YOUR LIFE, LAD - FOLLOW ME!

THE PACE WAS DEADLY, AND MY HEART SEEMED LIKE IT WOULD BURST AGAINST MY RIBS. BUT ALAN DID NOT SLACKEN, AND I FORCED MYSELF TO STAY WITH HIM.

AT LAST, HIGH IN THE WOOD, WE RESTED IN THE BRACKEN, AND I COULD VOICE THE THOUGHTS THAT TROUBLED ME...
I LIKED YOU VERY WELL, ALAN - BUT I CAN HAVE NO PART IN **COLD-BLOODED MURDER!**
AS ONE FRIEND TO ANOTHER, MR BALFOUR OF SHAWS...

IF I WERE GOING TO **KILL** A GENTLEMAN, I WOULD NOT DO IT IN MY **OWN** COUNTRY, TO BRING **TROUBLE** ON MY **CLAN**.
AND I WOULD TAKE A **SWORD** AND **GUN** - NOT A **FISHING ROD** ON MY BACK!

THEY'LL BE AFTER US BOTH NOW.
WE HAVE TO FLEE!
I HAVE NO FEAR OF THE JUSTICE OF MY OWN COUNTRY.
DAVIE, DAVIE! I WONDER AT YOUR INNOCENCE.

A **CAMPBELL** HAS BEEN KILLED. WE'LL BE TRIED IN **INVERARA**, THE CAMPBELL **CAPITAL**, WITH **FIFTEEN** CAMPBELLS ON THE **JURY** AND THEIR **DUKE** AS THE **JUDGE**.
WE'LL GET THE **SAME** JUSTICE THE **RED FOX** GOT AT THAT ROADSIDE!

EITHER TAKE TO THE HEATHER WITH ME - AN **OUTLAW** - OR **HANG** LIKE A DOG!
PUT LIKE THAT, ALAN, IT'S NO CHOICE AT ALL!

As we journeyed, Alan told me how the COVENANT had finally SUNK, and how he had escaped from Hoseason and the other survivors...

Alan had intended us to HIDE OUT at James of the Glens' home, but the murder of the Red Fox had CHANGED everything...
THE REDCOATS WILL BE SWARMING HERE TOMORROW! WE WILL NEED TO TRAVEL ON.

They fed us, and clothed us, but...
IT'S A SORRY BUSINESS, ALAN.
IF THEY SEEK YOU, THEY WILL SEEK ME. I HAVE ONLY ONE ESCAPE...
I MUST PUT OUT A REWARD UPON YOU!

Alan's MONEY BELT had been sent on by other means. So, furnished with swords and pistols, oatmeal and brandy - with rewards upon our outlaw heads! - we were ready for THE HEATHER.

DAY FOUND US IN A PRODIGIOUS VALLEY, STREWN WITH ROCKS AND WHERE RAN A FOAMING RIVER. WILD MOUNTAINS STOOD AROUND IT; THERE GREW THERE NEITHER GRASS NOR TREES.
I HAVE SOMETIMES THOUGHT SINCE THEN THAT IT MAY HAVE BEEN THE VALLEY CALLED GLENCOE, WHERE THE MASSACRE HAD BEEN IN THE NAME OF KING WILLIAM.
IT WAS A BARREN AND AN EERIE PLACE, TRULY A GLEN OF SORROW.

AND IT IS THANKS ONLY TO PROVIDENCE WE WERE NOT A MOMENT TOO SOON...

COME NIGHT, WE'LL SLIP DOWN AND GET BY THEM.
AND WHAT ARE WE TO DO TILL NIGHT?

COOK, DAVIE. WE'RE GOING TO BAKE LIKE TATTIE SCONES IN THAT SUN!

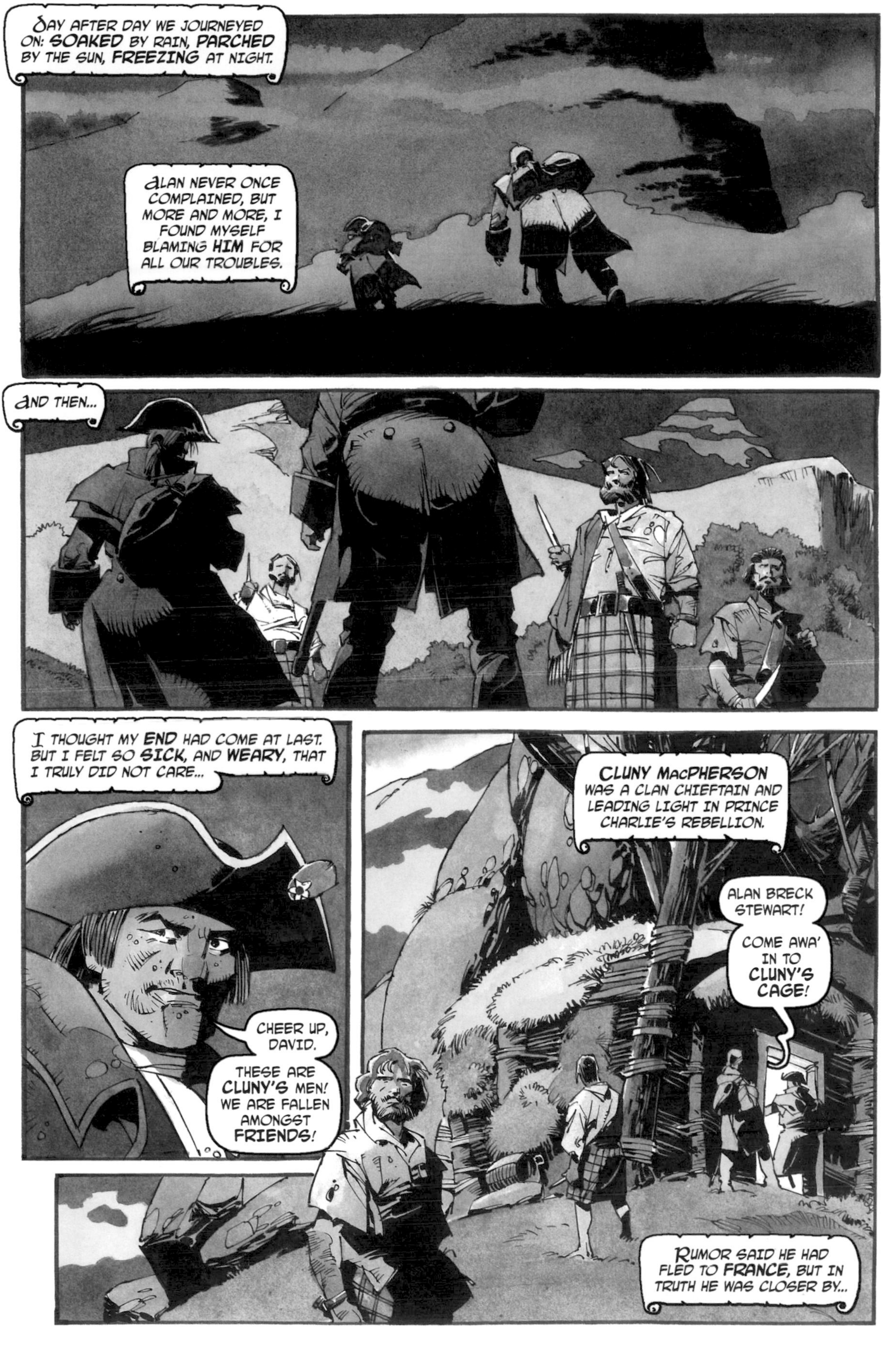

I THOUGHT MY END HAD COME AT LAST. BUT I FELT SO SICK, AND WEARY, THAT I TRULY DID NOT CARE...

CHEER UP, DAVID.

THESE ARE CLUNY'S MEN! WE ARE FALLEN AMONGST FRIENDS!

CLUNY MacPHERSON WAS A CLAN CHIEFTAIN AND LEADING LIGHT IN PRINCE CHARLIE'S REBELLION.

ALAN BRECK STEWART!

COME AWA' IN TO CLUNY'S CAGE!

RUMOR SAID HE HAD FLED TO FRANCE, BUT IN TRUTH HE WAS CLOSER BY...

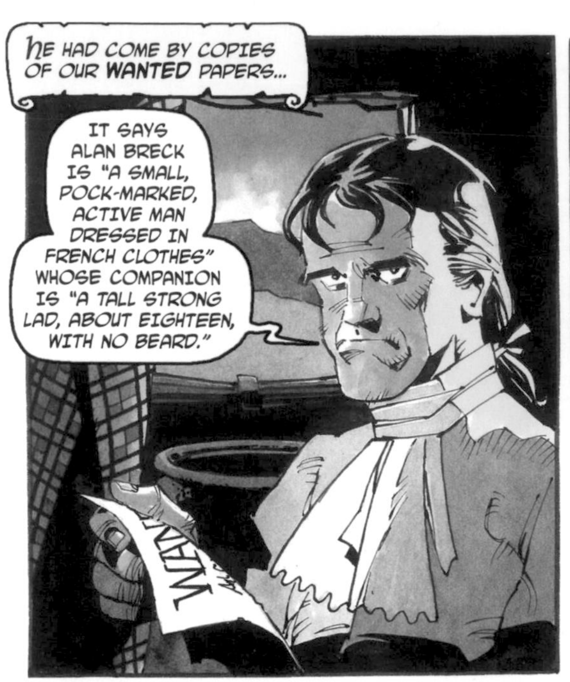
HE HAD COME BY COPIES OF OUR WANTED PAPERS...
IT SAYS ALAN BRECK IS "A SMALL, POCK-MARKED, ACTIVE MAN DRESSED IN FRENCH CLOTHES" WHOSE COMPANION IS "A TALL STRONG LAD, ABOUT EIGHTEEN, WITH NO BEARD."

DESPITE FOOD AND DRINK I FELT WEAK AND FEVERED. I TOOK TO BED, WHILE ALAN AND CLUNY PLAYED CARDS...

I WOKE, AND SLEPT, AND SLEPT AND WOKE, AND ALL SEEMED TO BE SOME STRANGE DREAM...
DAVID - I NEED TO BORROW YOUR MONEY. ALL RIGHT, LAD?
I... I SUPPOSE SO...

WHEN AT LAST I FELT RECOVERED, IT WAS ONLY TO FIND...
YE SHOULDNAE HAVE GIVEN ME YOUR MONEY, DAVIE! I'M DAFT WHEN IT COMES TO THE CARDS!
I'VE LOST THE LOT - AYE, AND MY OWN GOLD, TOO!

TO CUT A SORRY TALE SHORT, CLUNY GAVE ME BACK MY SHARE OF THE MONEY, THOUGH VERY RELUCTANTLY.
WHEN ALAN AND I LEFT HIS CAGE, WE COULD HARDLY BEAR TO SPEAK ONE WITH THE OTHER...

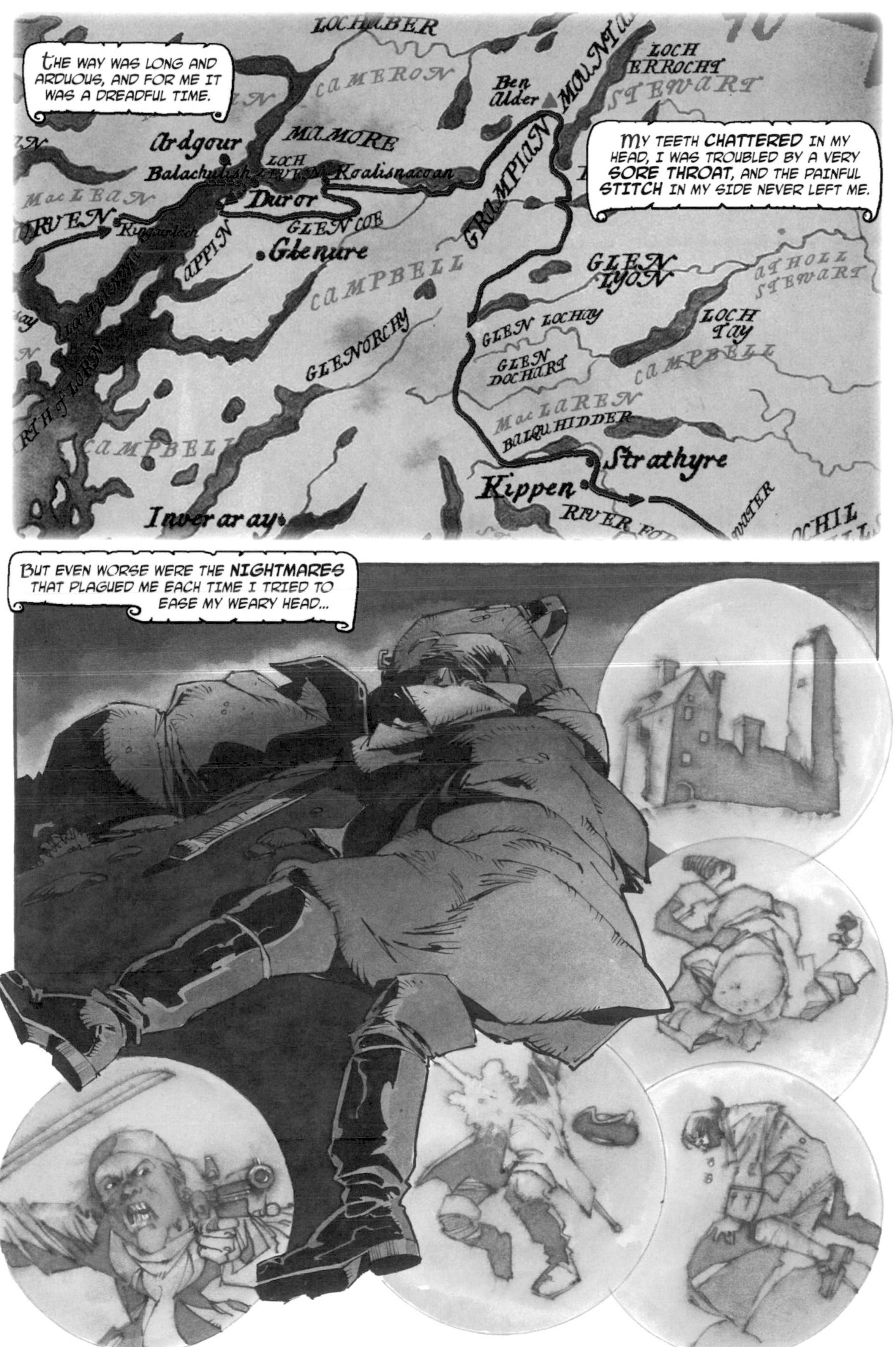

THE WAY WAS LONG AND ARDUOUS, AND FOR ME IT WAS A DREADFUL TIME.
MY TEETH **CHATTERED** IN MY HEAD, I WAS TROUBLED BY A VERY **SORE THROAT**, AND THE PAINFUL **STITCH** IN MY SIDE NEVER LEFT ME.
BUT EVEN WORSE WERE THE **NIGHTMARES** THAT PLAGUED ME EACH TIME I TRIED TO EASE MY WEARY HEAD...
LOCHABER
CAMERON
LOCH ERROCHT
Ben Alder
STEWART
Ardgour
MAMORE
Balachulish
Koalisnacoan
Duror
MacLEAN
Kingairloch
APPIN
GLEN COE
Glenure
GRAMPIAN
CAMPBELL
GLEN LYON
ATHOLL STEWART
GLEN LOCHAY
LOCH TAY
GLENORCHY
GLEN DOCHART
CAMPBELL
MacLAREN
BALQUHIDDER
Strathyre
Kippen
CAMPBELL
Inveraray
OCHIL

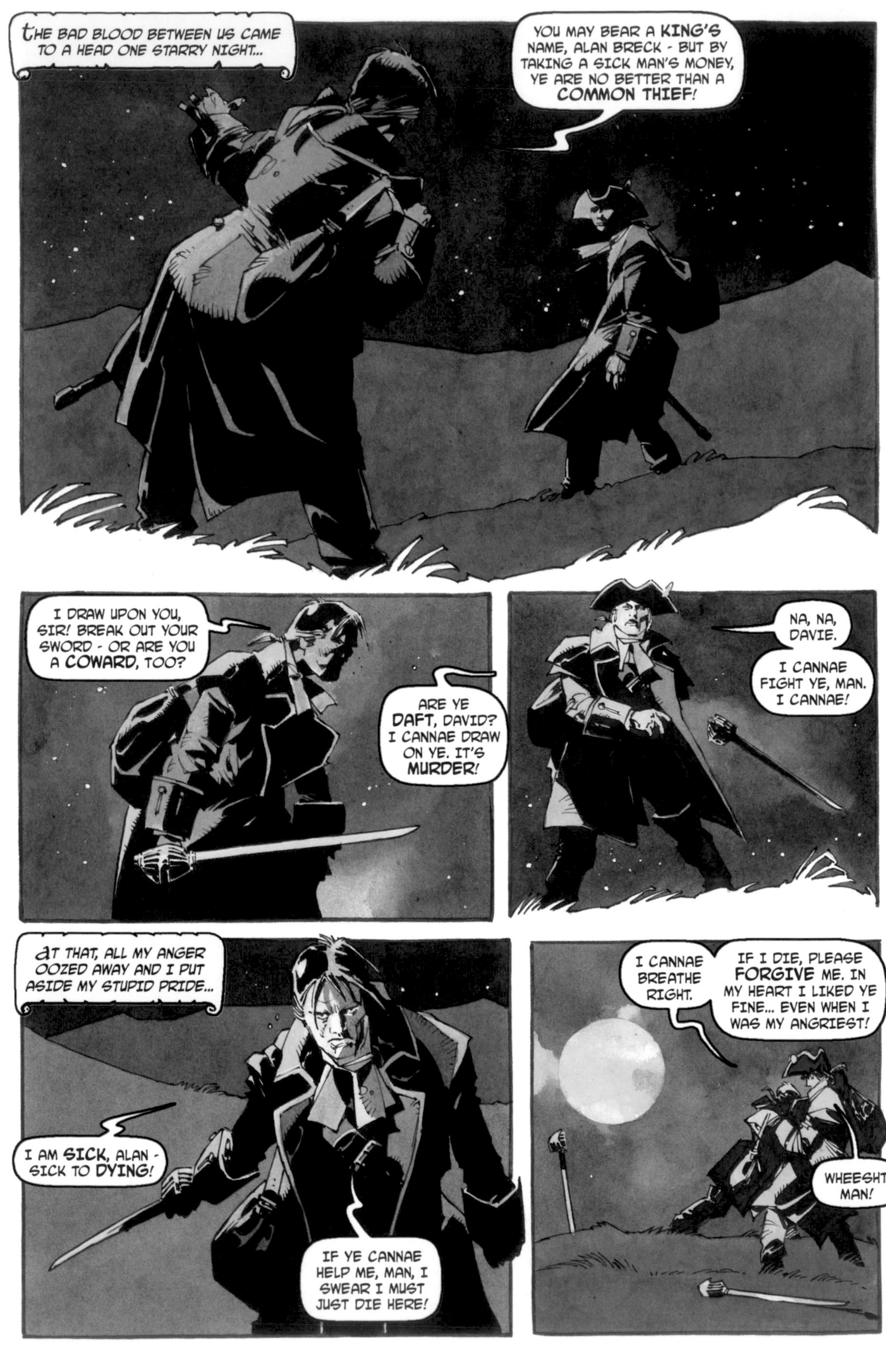

THE BAD BLOOD BETWEEN US CAME TO A HEAD ONE STARRY NIGHT...

YOU MAY BEAR A **KING'S** NAME, ALAN BRECK - BUT BY TAKING A SICK MAN'S MONEY, YE ARE NO BETTER THAN A **COMMON THIEF**!

YOU ARE MY FRIEND.
I WILL NOT LET YOU DIE!

WHAT MAKES YE SO GOOD TO ME, ALAN? WHAT MAKES YE CARE FOR SUCH A THANKLESS FELLOW?
THAT I DON'T KNOW.

FOR JUST PRECISELY WHAT I LIKED ABOUT YE, WAS THAT YE NEVER QUARRELLED.

AND NOW THAT YE DO - WHY, I LIKE YE EVEN BETTER!

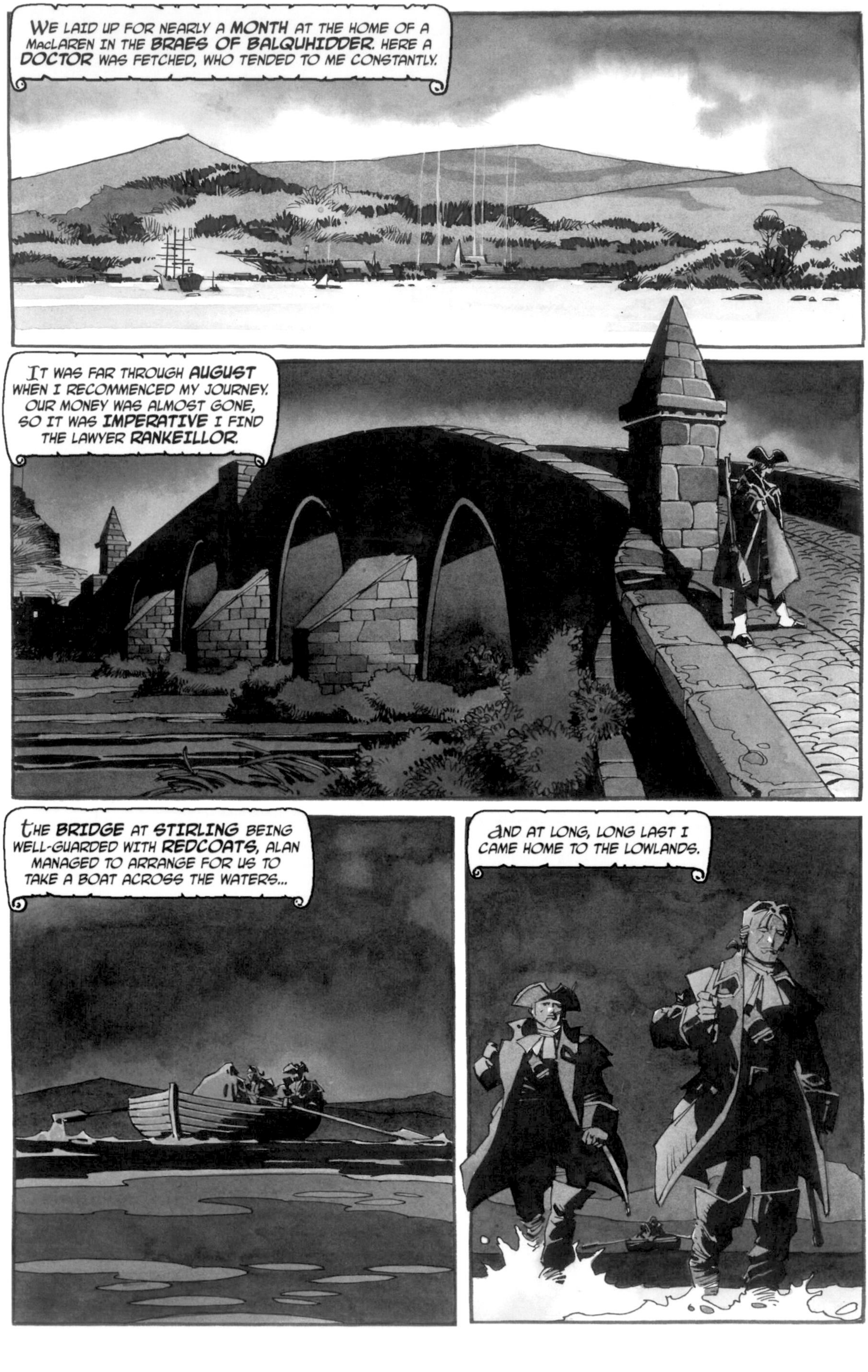

WE LAID UP FOR NEARLY A **MONTH** AT THE HOME OF A MacLAREN IN THE **BRAES OF BALQUHIDDER**. HERE A **DOCTOR** WAS FETCHED, WHO TENDED TO ME CONSTANTLY.

IT WAS FAR THROUGH **AUGUST** WHEN I RECOMMENCED MY JOURNEY. OUR MONEY WAS ALMOST GONE, SO IT WAS **IMPERATIVE** I FIND THE LAWYER **RANKEILLOR**.

It was decided Alan would hide near Newhalls, while I went to the Queen's Ferry in search of my uncle Ebenezer's lawyer, Rankeillor...
I told him the whole story, from the leaving of Essendean to my journey through the Highlands, leaving out nothing of my uncle's treachery...
TUT TUT! TO HAVE HIS OWN NEPHEW KIDNAPPED!

But when I came to mention Alan Breck...
I AM A MAN OF THE LAW, DAVID. I CANNOT COMPROMISE MY POSITION.
IF YOU MUST TALK OF OUTLAWS, THEN GIVE HIM ANOTHER NAME...
MR THOMSON, FOR INSTANCE.

SHAWS IS UNDOUBTEDLY YOURS, DAVID. BUT IF EBENEZER OBJECTS, IT WILL BE A HARD MATTER TO PROVE.
I THINK, SIR, THAT I MAY HAVE A SCHEME THAT WILL MAKE MY UNCLE CONFESS TO HIS MISDEEDS.

AND I SHALL NEED THE SERVICES OF MY FRIEND... MR THOMSON!

RANKEILLOR CAME WITH ME TO NEWHALLS, AND I WHISTLED THE SIGNAL THAT HAD BEEN AGREED...
WE TOLD ALAN - OR SHOULD I SAY, MR THOMSON - MY PLAN, AND ALL THREE OF US SET FORTH TO PLAY THE FINAL ACT...
NIGHT WAS FALLEN WHEN WE CAME IN VIEW OF THE HOUSE OF SHAWS. AS WE DREW NEAR, WE SAW NO GLIMMER OF LIGHT IN ANY PART OF THE BUILDING...
THE LAWYER AND I CREPT QUIETLY UP AND CROUCHED DOWN BESIDE THE CORNER OF THE HOUSE...
WHILE ALAN MARCHED UP AND BEGAN A THUND'ROUS KNOCKING ON THE DOOR...
EBENEZER BALFOUR! I WOULD HAVE WORDS WITH YOU!

THIS IS NAE TIME OF NIGHT FOR DECENT FOLK! WHAT BRINGS YE HERE?
I HAVE A BLUNDERBUSS, MIND!

I WOULD TALK ABOUT DAVID BALFOUR, SIR!

IT SEEMS A SHIP WENT DOWN OFF THE ISLE OF MULL, AND A SURVIVOR - THIS DAVID BALFOUR - FELL INTO THE HANDS OF MY KIN.
THEY HAVE HIM PRISONER IN AN AULD, RUINED CASTLE...

AND I FEAR THEY WILL DO HIM ILL UNLESS YOU HAVE MONEY TO PAY FOR HIM!

OCH, I'M NO' VERY CARING. HE WASNAE A GOOD LAD AT THE BEST OF IT, AND I'VE NAE CALL TO PAY A RANSOM!
WELL, SIR! YE'RE A HARD MAN, TO DESERT YOUR OWN BROTHER'S SON!

SO...DO YE WANT HIM KILLED - OR KEPT?

KEPT, SIR, KEPT! I'LL NOT SANCTION MURDER!

AND THAT WE DID. EBENEZER AGREED TO PAY ME TWO-THIRDS OF THE YEARLY INCOME AT SHAWS. SO THE BEGGAR HAD COME HOME, AND NOW I WAS A MAN OF MEANS AND HAD A NAME IN THE COUNTRY.

NEXT DAY, ALAN AND I WENT SLOWLY FORWARD, HAVING LITTLE HEART EITHER TO WALK OR SPEAK. WE WERE NEAR THE TIME OF OUR PARTING, AND REMEMBRANCE OF ALL THE BYGONE DAYS SAT UPON US SORELY.
WE CAME THE BY-WAY OVER THE HILL OF CORSTORPHINE, AND LOOKED DOWN ON THE BOGS AND OVER TO THE CITY AND THE CASTLE ON THE HILL. AND WE KNEW WE HAD COME TO WHERE OUR WAYS PARTED.

WE REPEATED ONCE AGAIN WHAT HAD BEEN AGREED: THE ADDRESS OF A STEWART LAWYER, AND THE HOUR AT WHICH ALAN MIGHT BE DAILY FOUND.
THEN WE STOOD A SPACE, AND LOOKED ON IN SILENCE.
WELL, GOODBYE.
GOODBYE.
NEITHER OF US LOOKED THE OTHER IN THE FACE, NOR DID I TAKE ONE BACK GLANCE AT THE FRIEND I WAS LEAVING...
BUT I FELT SO LOST AND LONESOME, THAT I COULD HAVE FOUND IT IN MY HEART TO SIT DOWN BY THE DYKE, TO CRY AND WEEP LIKE ANY BABY!

IT WAS COMING NEAR NOON WHEN I PASSED IN BY THE **WEST KIRK** AND THE **GRASSMARKET** INTO THE STREETS OF THE CAPITAL, WHERE RANKEILLOR HAD PLACED A **CREDIT** THAT MIGHT TAKE ALAN TO **SAFETY** IN **FRANCE**...

THE HUGE **HEIGHT** OF THE BUILDINGS, THE NARROW ARCHED **ENTRIES**, THE **HUBBUB** AND ENDLESS STIR... ALL STRUCK ME INTO A KIND OF **STUPOR** OF **SURPRISE**...

SO THAT I LET THE CROWD CARRY ME TO AND FRO.

YET ALL THE TIME WHAT I WAS THINKING OF WAS **ALAN** AT CORSTORPHINE.

AND ALL THE TIME THERE WAS A COLD **GNAWING** ON MY INSIDE, LIKE A **REMORSE** FOR SOMETHING **WRONG**.

THE HAND OF PROVIDENCE BROUGHT ME IN MY DRIFTING TO THE VERY DOOR OF THE **BRITISH LINEN COMPANY'S** BANK.

the end